T0315145

BOB SMALE

EXPLORING TRADE UNION IDENTITIES

Union Identity, Niche Identity and the Problem
of Organizing the Unorganized

BRISTOL
UNIVERSITY
PRESS

First published in Great Britain in 2020 by

Bristol University Press
University of Bristol
1-9 Old Park Hill
Bristol
BS2 8BB
UK
t: +44 (0)117 954 5940
www.bristoluniversitypress.co.uk

North America office:
Bristol University Press
c/o The University of Chicago Press
1427 East 60th Street
Chicago, IL 60637, USA
t: +1 773 702 7700
f: +1 773 702 9756
sales@press.uchicago.edu
www.press.uchicago.edu

© Bristol University Press 2020

British Library Cataloguing in Publication Data
A catalogue record for this book is available from the British Library.

Library of Congress Cataloging-in-Publication Data
A catalog record for this book has been requested.

ISBN 978-1-5292-0407-0 (hardback)
ISBN 978-1-5292-0409-4 (ePub)
ISBN 978-1-5292-0408-7 (ePDF)

The right of Bob Smale to be identified as author of this work has been asserted by him in accordance with the Copyright, Designs and Patents Act 1988.

All rights reserved: no part of this publication may be reproduced, stored in a retrieval system, or transmitted in any form or by any means, electronic, mechanical, photocopying, recording, or otherwise without the prior permission of Bristol University Press.

Every reasonable effort has been made to obtain permission to reproduce copyrighted material. If, however, anyone knows of an oversight, please contact the publisher.

The statements and opinions contained within this publication are solely those of the author and not of the University of Bristol or Bristol University Press. The University of Bristol and Bristol University Press disclaim responsibility for any injury to persons or property resulting from any material published in this publication.

Bristol University Press works to counter discrimination on grounds of gender, race, disability, age and sexuality.

Cover design by Blu Inc, Bristol
Front cover: image kindly supplied by Chuttersnap – Unsplash
Printed and bound in Great Britain by CPI Group (UK) Ltd, Croydon, CR0 4YY
Bristol University Press uses environmentally responsible print partners

To all those who have loved, encouraged and supported me
in my life and work.

Contents

List of Figures and Tables

List of Abbreviations

ACAS	Advisory, Conciliation and Arbitration Service
ACB	Association for Clinical Biochemistry and Laboratory Medicine
ACB/FCS	Association for Clinical Biochemistry and Laboratory Medicine/Federation of Clinical Scientists
ACFTU	All-China Federation of Trade Unions
AEP	Association of Educational Psychologists
AFL	American Federation of Labor
AFL–CIO	American Federation of Labor – Committee for Industrial Organization
AHDS	Association of Headteachers and Deputies in Scotland
ALCC	Association of Local Council Clerks
AMiE	Association of Managers in Education
APAP	Association of Professional Ambulance Personnel
APFO	Association of Principal Fire Officers
ASCL	Association of School and College Leaders
ASI	Association of Somerset Inseminators
ASLEF	Associated Society of Locomotive Engineers and Firemen
ASSU	Amateur and Semi-pro Sportsman's Union
ATL	Association of Teachers and Lecturers
AUE	Artists' Union England

AUT	Association of University Teachers
BACM–TEAM	British Association of Colliery Management – Technical Energy and Administrative Management
BADN	British Association of Dental Nurses
BAJ	British Association of Journalists
BALPA	British Air Line Pilots Association
BAPA	Belfast Airport Police Association
BAOT	British Association of Occupational Therapists Limited
BECTU	Broadcasting, Entertainment, Cinematograph and Theatre Union
BFAWU	Bakers Food and Allied Workers Union
BMA	British Medical Association
BOSTU	British Orthoptic Society Trade Union
BPA	Boots Pharmacists' Association
BSA	Bluechip Staff Association
BSU	Britannia Staff Union
BWA	Bus Workers Alliance
CAIWU	Cleaners and Allied Independent Workers Union
CBS	Confederation of British Surgery
CCP	Chinese Communist Party
CFDT	*Confédération Française Démocratique du travail* (French Democratic Confederation of Labour)
CFE–CGC	*Confédération Française de l'Encadrement – Confédération Générale des Cadres* (French Confederation of Management – General Confederation of Executives)
CFTC	*Confédération Française des Travailleurs Chrétiens* (French Confederation of Christian Workers)
CGB	*Christlicher Gewerkschaftsbund Deutschlands* (Christian Trade Union Confederation of Germany)

CGT	*Confédération Générale du Travail* (General Confederation of Labour)
CGT–FO	*Confédération Générale du Travail – Force Ouvrière* (General Confederation of Labour – Workers' Force)
CIO	Committee for Industrial Organization
CODP	College of Operating Department Practitioners
COHSE	Confederation of Health Service Employees
COP	College of Podiatry
CPD	continuing professional development
CSCSA	Currys Supply Chain Staff Association
CSP	Chartered Society of Physiotherapists
CTW	Change to Win
CUSCG	CU Staff Consultative Group
CWU	Communication Workers Union
DBB	*Deutscher Beamtenbund* (German Civil Service Federation)
DGB	*Deutscher Gewerkschaftsbund* (German Trade Union Confederation)
DGU	Driver and General Union
EFWU	Equality for Workers Union
EIS	Educational Institute of Scotland
EMA	Engineers and Managers Association
ESOSTU	European SOS Trade Union
FBU	Fire Brigades Union
FCS	Federation of Clinical Scientists
FDA	Association of First Division Civil Servants (FDA is the certified name)
FNV	*Federatie Nederlandse Vakbeweging* (Federation of Dutch Trade Unions)
FOA	Fire Officers Association
FPRS	Federation of Professional Railway Staff
FRSA	Fire and Rescue Services Association
FSU	Financial Services Union

GFTU	General Federation of Trade Unions
GMB	General, Municipal, Boilermakers and Allied Trade Union (GMB is now the certified name)
GMBATU	General Municipal, Boilermakers and Allied Trades Union
ICTU	Irish Congress of Trade Unions
IDU	Independent Democratic Union
IFNS	Independent Federation of Nursing in Scotland
INTO	Irish National Teachers' Organisation
IOJ	Institute of Journalists
IPMS	Institution of Professionals, Managers and Specialists
ISU	ISU (ISU is the certified name)
IWU	Independent Workers Union
IWUGB	Independent Workers Union of Great Britain
IWW	Industrial Workers of the World
LBSCA	Leeds Building Society Colleague Association
LBSSA	Leeds Building Society Staff Association
LNFA	Lough Neagh Fishermen's Association
LTU	Lloyds Trade Union
MOD	Ministry of Defence
MSF	Manufacturing, Science and Finance Union
MU	Musicians Union
NACO	National Association of Co-operative Officials
NACODS	National Association of Colliery Overmen, Deputies and Shotfirers
NAHT	National Association of Head Teachers
NALGO	National and Local Government Officers' Association
NARS	National Association of Racing Staff
NASS	National Association of Stable Staff
NASUWT	National Association of Schoolmasters and Union of Women Teachers

NAS	National Association of Schoolmasters
NATFHE	National Association of Teachers in Further and Higher Education
NCOA	National Crime Officers Association
NEU	National Education Union
NGSU	Nationwide Group Staff Union
NISPA	Northern Ireland Public Service Alliance
NSEAD	National Society for Education in Art and Design
NUJ	National Union of Journalists
NUM	National Union of Mineworkers
NUMAST	National Union of Marine, Aviation and Shipping Transport Officers
NUPE	National Union of Public Employees
NUS	National Union of Seamen
NUT	National Union of Teachers
PCS	Public and Commercial Services Union
PCU	Psychotherapy and Counselling Union
PDA	Pharmacists Defence Association (PDA Union is the certified name)
PFA	Professional Footballers Association
PGTU	Poole Greyhound Trainers Union
POA	Prison Officers Association
PPSA	Palm Paper Staff Association
PPU	Professional Pilots Union (PPU is the certified name)
PTSC	PTSC (PTSC is the certified name)
RCM	Royal College of Midwives
RCN	Royal College of Nursing
RCTU	R&C Trade Union (R&C Trade Union is the certified name)
RFU	Retained Firefighters Union
RMT	National Union of Rail, Maritime, and Transport Workers

ROA	Retired Officers Association
SABB	Staff Association of the Bank of Baroda (UK region)
SAU	Scottish Artists Union
SCEBTA	Scottish Colliery Enginemen, Boilermen and Tradesmen's Association
SCP	Society of Chiropodists and Podiatrists
SGSA	Shield Guarding Staff Association
SIT	social identity theory
SOR	Society of Radiographers
SSTA	Scottish Secondary Teachers' Association
STUC	Scottish Trades Union Congress
SUD–Rail	*Solidaire Unitaire et Démocratique – Rail* (Solidarity, Unity and Democracy–Rail)
SUE	Society of Union Employees (Unison)
SUWBBS	Staff Union West Bromwich Building Society
SWU	Social Workers Union
TGWU	Transport and General Workers Union
TSSA	Transport Salaried Staffs' Association
TUC	Trades Union Congress
UCAC	*Undeb Cenedlaethol Athrawon Cymru* (National Association of Teachers in Wales)
UCATT	Union of Construction, Allied Trades and Technicians
UCSW	Union of Country Sports Workers
UCU	University and College Union
UFS	Union of Finance Staff (UFS was the certified name prior to merger)
UIU	United and Independent Union
Unifi	Union for the Finance Industry
USDAW	Union of Shop Distributive and Allied Workers
UTU	Ulster Teachers Union
UVW	United Voices of the World

UWT	Union of Women Teachers
WEU	Workers of England Union
WGGB	Writers' Guild of Great Britain
WISA	Whatman International Staff Association
WRPA	Welsh Rugby Players' Association
WSA	Whatman Staff Association
YISA	Yorkshire Independent Staff Association

Notes on the Author

Bob Smale's interest in trade unionism stems from joining both the musicians' and bank employees' unions as a teenager, later taking a full-time secondment to BIFU (Banking, Insurance and Finance Union) before studying at Ruskin College and the University of Kent. He subsequently spent 31 years working in education, completing a doctorate with the University of Portsmouth and remaining active in the University and College Union (UCU) until retirement from University of Brighton in 2018. His scholarly interests include industrial relations and pedagogy. He is the lead author of *How to Succeed at University* (Smale and Fowlie, 2009, 2015) and sole author of *Manage Your Money* (2019), both for Sage Publications.

Acknowledgements

I want to put on record my thanks to all those who helped and supported me over the years in conducting the research and developing the new theoretical framework introduced in this book. In particular I want to acknowledge the trade union officials who completed questionnaires, participated in research interviews and generally answered questions during the course of the research; Ed Sweeney, the former chair of ACAS (Advisory, Conciliation and Arbitration Service); Stephen Williams, Peter Scott and Derek Adam Smith who supervised my doctoral research together with the support of many other staff at the University of Portsmouth. Finally many former colleagues at the University of Brighton for their help and support, including David Lain, Julie Fowlie, Carolyn Lewis, Jackie O'Reilly, Mark Hughes, Chris Matthews and lastly Jo Lucas, who transcribed all the research interviews.

Preface

At some point while studying at Ruskin College my tutor gave me the following essay title, 'Given the success of the Transport and General Workers Union, why does Britain need more than one union?' Although I can't now remember what my essay concluded, the question provoked a line of thinking which led to this book. While UK trade unions started in trades, later developing general and industrial forms, it is general unions that now predominate in membership. However, the vast majority of unions certified in Great Britain are not general and project a variety of identities, raising critical questions that this book addresses. These include explaining the diverse identities projected by contemporary trade unions, the primacy of general unions, the persistence of what are termed 'niche unions' in this work and the efficacy of this complex array of identities in recovering unions lost power and influence, restoring lost membership and organizing the unorganized.

Introduction

The purpose of this book is to take a fresh look at trade unions by focusing upon their identities and exploring what in this work is termed 'niche unionism'. While media and politicians frequently refer to *the unions* as if they were homogeneous, even the most rudimentary exploration of union names reveals that they project an extremely diverse range of identities. Although UK trade union membership decline has largely halted over recent years, unions seem to be making limited progress in recruiting beyond their traditional membership territories. While new and existing unions are making some inroads into the problem of organizing the unorganized, UK unions' age profile shows a preponderance of older members, leaving the vast majority of younger workers unorganized (BEIS, 2019), and raising important issues for union organization (Tailby and Pollert, 2011; Hodder, 2015). The result is that more than three-quarters of UK workers are unrepresented and, for the most part, UK unions remain cornered within relatively secure niches within the labour market. This then raises questions as to the relative effectiveness of contemporary union identities in helping to reverse union fortunes by organizing the unorganized.

Despite considerable discussion of union decline and renewal in recent decades (Blanchflower and Bryson, 2009; Brown et al, 2009; Simms and Charlwood, 2010; Simms et al, 2013;

Simms et al, 2019), there has been relatively little consideration of contemporary union identities (Hyman, 1994, 2001; Hodder and Edwards, 2015). This book argues that the extant industrial relations literature is inadequate and introduces a new approach to understanding individual union identities based upon the systematic observation and analysis of the characteristics through which unions project their identities in the public domain. The discussion also draws upon literature from intellectual traditions beyond the field of industrial relations, including organizational identity theory and marketing, where these are seen to inform the understanding of union identities and the significance of niche identity to trade unions. In doing so the work recognizes that trade unions are in essence organizations that can be seen as having much in common with other forms of organization, both in relation to projecting organizational identities and, in the majority of cases, projecting niche identities.

The research reveals that individual union identities draw upon a limited number of sources and that unions certified in Great Britain are now broadly divided between those projecting general identities and those which have adopted or retained some niche characteristics. It further recognizes that whereas trade union mergers frequently lead to loss of identity, and particularly so where niche unions merge with general unions, new unions often organize niche memberships and, despite a high attrition rate, provide an alternative route to organizing the unorganized. The work introduces the concept of 'niche unionism' which encompasses both 'niche unions' that organize discrete areas within the labour market and larger, and particularly general unions that organize niches through occupational or industrial sections. The work considers issues influencing the development of union identities and niche unionism and the efficacy of these in relation to organizing unorganized workers. However, because the research explores projected identities it does not focus on the perception of union identities by existing or potential members, which would require alternative approaches

The findings are based upon systematic research and analysis conducted with the aims of increasing the understanding of trade union identities and the role of niche and stimulating debate, particularly on the problem of organizing the unorganized. Identification of the sources of union identity facilitated the construction of a multidimensional framework of analysis which allows individual unions to be plotted against the sources of their identity. Because the framework is flexible in application it avoids the rigidity of strict categorization which can lead to error by grouping dissimilar unions together under broad headings. However, the multidimensional framework is not presented as a universal panacea for the understanding of all trade unions, at all times and in all places, but rather as a flexible framework that is capable of development to reflect future realities. While the research originated in, and is largely focused upon unions certified in Great Britain, it is recognized that certain unions based in Northern Ireland are certified there under separate arrangements (see Chapter Six). The book also briefly considers the manifestation of union identities and niche unionism in other countries and suggests how the multidimensional framework could be developed for use in locations where additional sources of identity are required (see Chapter Eight).

As regards the structure of the book, Chapter One first considers why it is important to understand trade union identities and what is wrong with existing theoretical approaches. Chapter Two introduces the multidimensional framework for the analysis of trade union identities and niche union identity. Chapters Three to Six look in turn at general, industrial/ occupational, organizational and geographical unions, asking critical questions as to the efficacy of these identities. Chapter Seven discusses the developing story of union identities and niche unionism including the impact of mergers, rebranding, new unions and union dissolutions. Chapter Eight considers how the multidimensional framework and the concept of niche unionism might be applied in other countries. Finally, Chapter Nine draws together what has been learnt from the research and then turns to consider critical questions that emerged from it for the future of union identities and niche unionism and the implications of these for the future of union organization and the problem of organizing the unorganized.

ONE

What's the Problem?

Introduction

This works starts from the position that trade unions, as with other organizations, project distinct identities through which they can be recognized in the public domain and the contention that through better understanding trade union identities we can better understand the trade union movement today and who it seeks to represent. With UK unions now representing less than a quarter of the workforce (BEIS, 2019) and making limited progress in organizing the unorganized, it is argued here that developing a better understanding of union identities can make an important contribution to wider debates on union revitalization. Therefore this chapter looks first at the development of trade union identities, the impact of change in recent decades and the case for developing a new understanding of trade union identities while recognizing the phenomenon termed 'niche unionism' in this work. It identifies four drivers towards identity change in trade unions, namely union mergers, rebranding and the formation of new unions and the dissolution of existing ones (see further discussion of these drivers in Chapter Seven). This chapter first reviews the limitations of industrial relations literature in explaining both trade union identities and niche unionism, before considering contributions from disciplines beyond the industrial relations silo, including organization theory and marketing.

Why is it important to understand union identities?

In search of a starting point for the development of trade union identities, it can be seen that UK trade unions originated largely in crafts and were bounded by occupational and geographical membership territories (Turner, 1962). With the development of successful general unions and later industrial unions there developed a structure of union organization which Clegg (1979, p 174) describes as 'bizarre and complex'. Staff associations developed separately within companies, frequently with the encouragement of employers as part of trade union avoidance strategies. Many of these unions progressed to achieve a certificate of independence and some to merge with more broadly based trade unions, which might be seen as a 'direction of travel' (see further discussion in Chapter Five). However, trade union development in the UK, as in other countries, has for the most part been limited to national boundaries (see further discussion in Chapter Six).

While it is beyond the purpose of this work to rehearse the dramatic decline of union power and influence over recent decades, the decline can be seen as an important driver towards changes in union identities. With UK trade union membership now less than half of that reported at its peak four decades ago (BEIS, 2019) and with the number of unions reduced to less than a third over the same period (Certification Officer, 2019a), many unions have merged and/or adopted new identities. One result is that UK union membership is now divided between general unions and those which have adopted or retained some element of what is called in this work a 'niche identity'. Although membership decline has either slowed or shown limited gains in recent years (BEIS, 2019), unions seem to be making limited progress in recruiting beyond their traditional membership territories. The result is that more than three-quarters of UK workers remain unrepresented (Pollert, 2010) and that many unions remain largely cornered within relatively secure niches in the labour market. This raises a question as to how well positioned unions are to organize the unorganized. If we pose a question as to how unorganized workers might know which is the most appropriate union for them to join, the answer can be problematic. While many unions, such as the Professional Footballers Association (PFA) or Musicians Union (MU) have retained clear identities, some such as Accord and Unite have adopted 'aspirational' titles which give no indication of who they might represent (Gall, 2007; Balmer, 2008). As demonstrated later in this work, the problem of establishing who a union actually organizes frequently requires a deeper investigation of their websites.

From time to time new unions are formed and despite their high attrition rate they may provide an alternative route to organizing the unorganized. Whereas trade union mergers often lead to some dilution of identity, and particularly so where niche unions merge with general unions, new unions frequently organize niche memberships. The formation of a number of what are termed in this work 'new-generation' unions, such as the IWUGB (Independent Workers Union of Great Britain), may herald a new approach to organizing precarious workers. This raises questions both as to the efficacy of existing union identities and the potentialities for the future development of new unions. Despite new and existing unions making some inroads into the 'gig economy', the age profile of UK unions clearly shows a preponderance of older members with the result that the vast majority of younger workers are unorganized (BEIS, 2019). This has raised academic interest in both the propensity of young workers to join trade unions and the relative success of union recruitment (Tailby and Pollert, 2011; Hodder, 2015; see further discussions in Chapters Seven and Nine).

What is clear is that having developed a complex array of union identities, experienced severe membership loss, successive merger waves, extensive rebranding and the formation of new unions, unions are having limited success in organizing the unorganized. It therefore seems imperative to develop a systematic understanding of the identities which unions are projecting in the public domain in order to consider how they might improve their appeal to a more significant proportion of the working population and more effectively organize the unorganized.

What is wrong with existing theoretical approaches?

While much industrial relations literature is devoted to understanding aspects of trade unions, there is relatively little direct reference to the question of identity. Contributions that inform this discussion fall under two broad headings that can be described as the 'categorizers' (Webb and Webb, 1894, 1902, 1920; Hughes, 1967; Hyman, 1975; Clegg, 1979; Heery and Kelly, 1994; Visser, 2012) and those who employ more flexible approaches (Turner, 1962; Blackburn 1967; Undy et al, 1981; Hyman, 1994, 2001; Hodder and Edwards, 2015). Although categorization is used widely in social sciences, the problem is that it inevitably involves forcing the individual instances into boxes within which they may not comfortably fit. As is demonstrated later in this book, union identities are frequently constructed from a range of sources, making categorization unsatisfactory. Therefore it is argued here that categorization is too rigid and that a more flexible approach is required.

The Webbs (1894, 1902, 1920) provide a starting point for the discussion of union identities with their rudimentary distinction of craft unions from their 'New Model' and the later general unions. In their enthusiasm for the 'New Model' (Allen, 1963; Hobsbawm, 1967), they tended to underestimate the later phenomenon of 'new unionism' (Allen, 1963; Musson, 1976), which provided the foundations for modern general unionism. However, the Webbs' (1894) 'New Model' is more significant for this work in being based on the observation of characteristics. Hyman (1975, p 38) uses the established categorizations of 'craft', 'industrial' and 'general', while Clegg (1979) drew on Hughes (1967), who introduced two additional categories of 'sector' and 'sector-general' unions. Somewhat surprisingly Clegg (1979 then suggests that they are of limited value because of the complex structure of British trade unionism. It is argued here that these additional categories might now be considered largely redundant because many of the unions categorized as sector and sector-general unions have been absorbed into general unions (Waddington, 1995; Undy, 2008; McIlroy and Daniels, 2009). As regards those such unions that remain, they can be identified by some combination of industry and occupation, albeit in variable measures (see Chapter Four).

In contrast, Heery and Kelly (1994) introduced a threefold typology to explain trends in union development focused primarily on the functions of unions and suggests that in 'professional' unions activity is led by full-time officials, whereas in 'participative' unions members are encouraged towards self-reliance in leading activity, and in 'managerial' unions members are viewed as reactive consumers. The function and modus operandi of individual unions are not of necessity unrelated to how unions are perceived, as is recognized in organizational identity theory (Albert and Whetten, 1985; Balmer, 2008; see further discussion later in this chapter). However, the work of Heery and Kelly (1994) can be criticized primarily because of an over-focus on servicing relationships at the expense of other salient factors (Smith, 1995), and for the methodological limitations of adopting a limited typology (Ackers, 1995). It is therefore argued here that while Heery and Kelly (1994) provide useful insight into unions' internal servicing relationships, they do not provide a comprehensive explanation of unions' projected identities, which are the focus of this work.

More recently, Visser (2012, p 18), writing in a European context, introduced a fivefold typology comprising: blue-collar sectorial; narrow sectorial organizing non-manual workers or white-collar staff; blue-collar craft union; occupational white-collar; and general. Any attempt to apply this typology to UK trade unions beyond the 'general' and 'occupational white-collar' categories is problematic given the tendency of many blue-collar unions to have merged, albeit sometimes in stages, into general unions (Waddington, 1995; Undy, 2008). While there are unions which are either predominantly blue-collar, such as RMT (National Union of Rail, Maritime, and Transport Workers) or white-collar, as exemplified by Prospect, it is suggested here that Visser's (2012) typology is only applicable on a piecemeal basis in the UK and is therefore of limited use in understanding contemporary UK union identities.

Turning to look at flexible frameworks which allow for the relative strength of various criteria to be considered, Turner's (1962) seminal work recognizes unions as being relatively more 'open' or 'closed', effectively setting up a continuum. Towards the closed end he argues that early craft unions were based upon exclusivity and dependent upon their ability to control entry and enforce the standard rate, which can be seen as an expression of 'occupational closure' (Weber, 1978). Rejecting simple categorization, Turner (1962, p 233) suggests that terms such as 'craft', 'occupational', 'industrial' and 'general' 'may sometimes indicate the union's ... original shape'. In contrast, towards the open end of the continuum, Turner (1962, p 221) questions the relative openness of general unions, stating: 'Old unions prevented them becoming truly general organisations'. While Turner's (1962) achievement is to produce a framework capable of application to all unions, its limitation is that a single dimension cannot explain the complex construction of contemporary unions' projected identities. The concepts of union identities, niche union identity and niche unionism explored in this work do not therefore stand in opposition to Turner's (1962) work, but rather seek to extend it. The question for this book is, therefore, 'what does closed mean in terms of contemporary union identities and how does this help us to understand niche unionism?'

In contrast to the simplicity of Turner's (1962) open/closed continuum, Blackburn (1967), Undy et al (1981), Hyman (1994, 2001) and Hodder and Edwards (2015) offer more complex frameworks of analysis. Blackburn's (1967) concept of 'unionateness' employs seven 'elements' used to determine how 'union-like' unions are. While the first three are relative concepts, the last three are absolute, and the fourth falls between the two. Although his selection of elements is open to potential criticism, the value of his approach for this work lies in the adoption of a multidimensional approach. As some of these elements could be considered as aspects of union identity, the relevance of his elements to this work are considered here at some length.

Blackburn's (1967) first element relates to the importance of collective bargaining and the protection of members' interests but has reduced in importance as a result of the decline in collective bargaining activity over recent decades (Brown et al, 2009). Blackburn's (1967) second and fifth elements, independence from the employer and registration as a trade union, have to some extent been overtaken by the legislative requirement for unions to demonstrate independence in order to achieve certification. As independence is a relative element for Blackburn (1967), two issues should be mentioned here. The first relates to those unions originating as in-house staff associations that have achieved certification, including Advance, (formerly the Abbey National Staff Association) and Accord (formerly the Halifax Building Society Staff Association), together with those which have merged with certified unions (Gall, 1997, 2001). This suggests a 'direction of travel' towards independence and that certification may be an important stage in establishing union identity (Ross, 2013). However, the public record reports 12 'unlisted' organizations observed to be operating 'within the statutory definition of a trade union' (Certification Officer, 2019a, p 24). Beyond this there are others, such as the Police Federation of England and Wales, which represents the lower ranks of the police force individually and collectively, albeit without recourse to industrial action by statutory bar (Allen, 1958; Bean, 1980; Seifert and Mather, 2013). Therefore, while this study is limited to certified unions, it is recognized that there are other organizations which may project a trade union identity.

Blackburn's (1967) third element, propensity to militancy, which may now be less relevant given the substantial decline in industrial action over recent decades (Dix et al, 2009; Lyddon, 2009). However, it is recognized here that certain unions such as FBU (Fire Brigades Union), PCS (Public and Commercial Services Union) and RMT have attracted a militant reputation which might form part of their identities (Connelly and Darlington 2012; Darlington, 2012; Taylor and Moore, 2015). However, with so much of the UK's membership now contained within general unions, the position is more complex. For example, it can be questioned whether Unite is a moderate or militant union, given that the union was involved in a long and bitter dispute with British Airways (Taylor and Moore, 2015) but held a partnership agreement with Barclays Bank (Wills, 2004). It is therefore argued that unions may be both moderate and militant on a piecemeal, opportunistic or pragmatic basis, making militancy or moderation a problematic component of their identities.

Blackburn's (1967, p 33) fourth element concerns whether a union declares itself as such and relates to a union's 'perception of itself, and the public image it wishes to create'. This element is perhaps the one most closely related to the observation of union identities in this study and, as reported later in this work, some unions were observed either to be unclear or to avoid declaring their status as trade unions (see discussion of 'clandestine' unions in Chapter Two). A further factor that has changed since Blackburn (1967) wrote is the practice of unions such as Accord, Advance, Unite and Unison to adopt titles expressing aspiration rather than function (Gall, 2007;

Balmer, 2008), with the result that their union identity is not confirmed by their name alone.

Blackburn's (1967, p 37) sixth element is TUC (Trades Union Congress) affiliation, which he saw as providing, 'The most direct way of expressing shared interests and identity with other unions'. There are currently 48 affiliates (TUC, 2019), representing a little over a third of all unions certified in Great Britain (Certification Officer, 2019a). The TUC claims these contain 5.5 million members, representing 86.6 per cent of the membership of unions certified in Great Britain (BEIS, 2019; TUC, 2019). It may be interesting to note here that the Trade Disputes and Trade Unions Act (1927), a piece of reactive legislation initiated by Baldwin's Conservative government following the 1926 General Strike, and repealed by the post-war Labour government in 1946, barred civil service unions from affiliating to the TUC and from pursuing political objectives (Taylor, 2000). However, TUC affiliates now include Association of First Division Civil Servants (FDA), PCS and other unions representing civil servants, forming a significant proportion of its affiliated membership. Whereas Blackburn (1967, p 38), suggests that affiliation is 'always a potential source of controversy in white-collar unions' and that 'White-collar workers' objections to the TUC are frequently political', these contentions now seem less relevant, with many TUC affiliates being dominated by non-manual workers. However, with almost two-thirds of certified unions currently outside the TUC, albeit containing a minority of union members, there is a need to explain the relevance of TUC affiliation to union identity (see later discussion of NARS [National Association of Racing Staff] in Chapter Four and Advance in Chapter Five).

Blackburn's (1967) seventh element is Labour Party affiliation and while the three largest general unions remain fully or partially affiliated to the Labour Party, only 12 unions in total are currently affiliated (Labour Party, 2019). Noticeable absentees include PCS and RMT, which are no strangers to political activity. Blackburn (1967) again raises the issue of white-collar reluctance, which is perhaps less relevant today as some of affiliated unions' membership is drawn from non-manual occupations, mostly through general union and other unions, with the Transport Salaried Staffs' Association (TSSA) and perhaps MU as the only clearly white-collar affiliates. A more useful distinction today might be with professional identity, as no affiliate could be described as a professional union. Although the New Labour period saw increasing distance between the unions and the party, the party's subsequent shift to the left may signal a change in the relationship. Therefore, the contemporary relevance of this element in the construction of union identity might be subject to change.

Overall, Blackburn's (1967) work on 'unionateness' is valuable both in avoiding categorization and in developing a multidimensional framework of analysis based upon a broad range of observable characteristics. While some of his elements are now less relevant measures of 'unionateness' and are not necessarily appropriate to an understanding of contemporary union identities, others, such as whether a union declares itself as such, a union's propensity to militancy together with TUC and Labour Party affiliation were considered worthy of consideration in this work.

Undy et al (1981), in seeking to explain change in trade unions, avoid categorization by setting up a number of criteria. Although their work is not directly relevant to the question of identity, it informed this investigation in seeking to understand a complex interaction of internal factors by employing a flexible framework of analysis while recognizing unions as being in a dynamic situation.

In contrast to other writers, Hyman (1975, 1994, 2001) employs different frameworks of analysis at different times to explain union identities. Despite generally recognizing the role of class, he followed established categories of union identity in earlier work (Hyman, 1975). Writing later in the context of European trade unionism he offers two differing, if at times overlapping, explanations of union identities (Hyman,

1994, 2001). Hyman (1994), suggests a four factor model in which union identity is a result of the interaction of 'interest', 'democracy', 'agenda' and 'power'. He argues that business unionism supplanted class unionism and cites factors including the restructuring of capital and the breakdown of manual and non-manual distinctions. In contrast, Hyman (2001) introduces an 'eternal triangle' of 'market', 'society' and 'class', within which the multiplicity of union forms can be located, arguing that, 'All unions face in three directions' (Hyman, 2001, p 3). He cites Perlman (1928, in Hyman, 2001), who contrasted American unions as being more concerned with employment issues and European unions as being more politicized. Hyman (2001) argues that in continental Europe it was the move to institutionalized relations with employers that led to an increasingly 'ritualistic' profession of class and a drift towards a form of business unionism and political reformism. As regards Britain, he concludes that 'Trends in British trade union identity remain uneven, uncertain and contested' and that 'experience since 1979 has clearly shaken the stability of trade unionism founded on the market class axis' (Hyman, 2001, p 110).

Several problems emerge in trying to apply Hyman's later frameworks to this work on the projected identities of contemporary trade unions (Hyman, 1994, 2001). Firstly, being conceived in a European context the frameworks are highly generalized to accommodate the diversity of unions operating within differing national structures. Secondly, because these frameworks are so generalized, there is very little to criticize in terms of the factors identified, but rather the problem is that both have limited value in developing a comprehensive understanding of the projected identities of contemporary unions. Finally, neither framework appears to be based upon any empirical research from which the relevant factors were derived and nor is it clear how they could be operationalized. Therefore it is argued that a more sophisticated framework of analysis is required to understand unions' projected identities, based upon the systematic collection and analysis of data on observable characteristics and the identification of sources of union identity.

More recently, Hodder and Edwards (2015, p 843) addressed the question of union identities within a wide-ranging theoretical discussion and suggest 'a framework to help understand the essence of trade unions'. They broadly follow the Marxian logic of base and superstructure in seeing trade union identities as reflective of the economic base of society. However, even if this is accepted, it does not explain the diversity of identities projected by trade unions in the UK and beyond. As with Hyman's (1994, 2001) later contributions, Hodder and Edwards' (2015) framework is generalized and lacks empirical justification. Further, it is unclear whether their framework relates to unions' projected identities as considered in this work or to the perception of trade unions, and if the latter, then by whom. Therefore it is argued here that it does not advance the understanding of certified unions' projected identities, nor does it provide a more convincing explanation than this work, which is based on detailed observation and analysis.

Theoretical support for the contribution of class to union identity is relatively limited (Lockwood, 1958; Blackburn, 1967; Hyman, 2001; Hodder and Edwards, 2015). Hyman (1994) omits class in his earlier framework only for it to emerge in his later contribution (Hyman, 2001). Hodder and Edwards (2015, p 850) include 'degree of class focus' as an element in their 'essence of unions framework', although it is not clear how this could be assessed. In search of empirical evidence, Moore (2011), exploring the role of class consciousness in workplace organization, found that only half her sample of workplace representatives considered themselves to be working class. However, with participants being drawn exclusively from general and industrial unions and with none from organizational or professional unions, the sample is somewhat skewed and may therefore overestimate class consciousness. Holgate (2013), exploring community unionism, and Tapia (2013), recognizing the problems of mobilization, draw attention to community organization and provide evidence of new forms of class-based unionism. While these contributions suggest that class remains an issue in understanding UK trade unions, evidence for the contribution of class to the construction of union identities is inconclusive and requires further investigation.

Overall this section demonstrates that existing theoretical approaches, while informing the discussion, do not adequately explain contemporary UK certified trade union identities. Categorization is problematic in that it inevitably leads to putting relatively dissimilar unions into a limited number of boxes into which they may not comfortably fit. Flexible frameworks are considered as being more appropriate because a number of factors can be considered in understanding an individual union's identity. However, all existing frameworks are considered to be largely inappropriate, outdated or inadequate for this purpose and therefore it is argued that because of the shortcomings of existing theorizations, a new approach is needed. Having considered the limitations of industrial relations literature, this chapter now turns to look at what can be learnt from other disciplines.

What is the contribution of organizational identity theories?

This section argues that organizational identity theory can contribute to understanding union identities. The field is multidisciplinary but draws primarily upon marketing, which tends to focus on the external perception of organizations, and on organizational behaviour, which concentrates more on the internal perceptions of members and employees (Balmer, 2008). Whetten (2006, p 221) suggests that organizations are 'more than social collectives' in having both legal and social identities, and emphasizes their uniqueness. If not unique, it is suggested here that unions project distinct identities which can be understood by the observation and analysis of certain 'observable characteristics'. Organizational identity theorists suggest that these characteristics should be 'central, enduring and distinctive' (Albert and Whetten, 1985; Whetton, 2006) and that it is the 'enduring attributes of an organization that distinguish it from other organizations' (Whetten, 2006, p 220). Similarly, Balmer (2008, p 886) suggests that, 'a corporate identity is characterised as having traits that are substantive and, whose effects are observable'. However, since the seminal work of Albert and Whetten (1985), questions have been raised as to the selection of criteria for observable characteristics and the potential for organizations to have multiple identities (He and Brown, 2013). This raises important questions for this work, which is limited to those characteristics observed to contribute to the construction of unions' identities that are projected in the public domain.

Balmer and Soenen developed four different conceptions of organizational identity which can be related to trade unions. 'Actual Identity' is what the organization actually is and is represented by, 'the values held by the staff and management of the organisation and how these values are concretely manifested' (Balmer and Soenen, 1999, p 83). Relating this to unions would require both members and activists to be included. 'Communicated Identity' relates to how the organization is perceived. 'Ideal Identity' 'refers to the optimal positioning the organisation can achieve in its market or markets' (Balmer and Soenen, 1999, p 83), which can be related to unions' membership territories. Finally, 'Desired Identity' refers to 'the management vision and the corporate mission of the organisation' (Balmer and Soenen, 1999, p 84), which can be related to the strategies and policies adopted by unions from time to time. The term 'projected identity' used in this work relates to Balmer and Soenen's (1999) 'ideal' and 'desired' identities, because these refer to areas of discretion regarding what unions say about themselves, how they define their membership territories and what they aspire to be, whereas their 'actual' and 'communicated' identities relate to perceptions that are beyond the scope of this study. The concept of discretion then raises an important question on the extent to which union identities are constructed. The contribution of design is highlighted by Balmer (1998), who points out the role of consultancy in facilitating the process, and by Balmer and Soenen (1999) when discussing corporate identity management. More recently, Burghausen and Balmer (2015) have discussed the concept of 'corporate heritage identity stewardship', which relates to the maintenance of past identity that is relevant to the present and future of the organization. These contributions raise important issues for unions certified in Great Britain, many of which have dispensed with historic identities, frequently through merger and/or by rebranding, while others have maintained their identities over time.

Organizational identity theories are recognized here as making two significant contributions to the understanding of trade union identities. Firstly, in acknowledging that organizations have observable characteristics which distinguish them from other organizations (Whetton, 2006; Balmer, 2008). Secondly, in recognizing that organizational identities can be actively managed (Balmer and Soenen, 1999) and maintained over time (Burghausen and Balmer, 2015). While organizational identity theories help to inform an understanding of union identities, they do not explain why unions adopt niche identities or practise niche unionism and therefore the next section turns to exploring theories which are instructive in understanding the question of niche.

What is the significance of niche to trade unions?

Although the vast majority of unions certified in Great Britain are not general in character and therefore restrict their membership to niches within the labour market, there is little consideration of niche in industrial relations literature (Hyman, 2001; Visser, 2012). The discussion therefore draws more heavily upon work in other disciplines, including ecology and marketing (Dalgic and Leeuw, 1994; Hannan et al, 2003); self-categorization theory and social identity theory (Ashforth and Mael, 1989; Hogg et al, 1990; Brown, 2000) and identity theory (Hogg et al, 1995).

The concept of niche organization is explored in the sociological context by Hannan et al, who cite Elton (1927, cited in Hannan et al, 2003) as the seminal writer, albeit within the field of ecology. Hannan et al (2003, p 312) suggest a model of niche organization as 'a market; an audience with members possessing distinctive tastes; a set of sociodemographic positions associated with the audience members; a set of organizations making offers; and organizations with identities and applicable organization-form codes', all of which might broadly be applied both to unions and those they seek to organize. Hannan et al (2003) also recognize the relative width of niches and that niches may overlap, which can be related to Turner's (1962) conceptualization of unions as being relatively more open or closed (discussed earlier in this chapter). Following the logic of the ecological model, Hannan et al (2003) highlight the fitness of organizations to survive in competitive situations. In this respect we can see that unions in a poor financial state are sometimes dissolved or forced into a defensive merger (Willman et al, 1993; Waddington, 1995; Undy, 2008; see discussions on union mergers and dissolutions in Chapter Seven).

The term 'niche' as used in marketing is defined by Dalgic and Leeuw (1994, p 40) as 'a small market consisting of an individual customer or a small group of customers with similar characteristics or needs'. This recognizes that the term applies to markets but not necessarily to organizations. They suggest that 'Small companies do not have a monopoly on niches but that they may be better focused and equipped to serve these markets in contrast to their big brothers' (Dalgic and Leeuw, 1994, p 44). Thus it is recognized in this work that whereas 'niche unions' organize defined niches within the labour market, the term 'niche unionism' also includes those unions serving multiple niches through sectionalized structures. Further, niches may overlap, some may be more competitive and smaller niche unions may be more vulnerable to change because of their niche identity. Dalgic and Leeuw (1994) suggest that organizations adopt a niche position to avoid competition and confrontation with larger organizations, to improve opportunity and for survival. In the case of unions, it may be that a niche identity is derived from a union's origins in an occupation, industry or organization (Turner, 1962; Webb and Webb, 1894, 1902, 1920; Hyman, 1975), or from the subsequent choice of merger partner (Waddington, 1995; Undy, 2008). However, Dalgic and Leeuw (1994) suggest that exploitation of a niche requires appropriate positioning of the product and differentiation from those of competitors. Relating this to unions it is argued that whereas some unions occupy niches relatively free from competition, such as those of most professional associations in the health sector, others are in a more competitive situation, as exemplified by the plethora of unions organizing in compulsory education (see further discussion in Chapter Four).

References to niche in industrial relations literature are limited to a passing reference by Hyman (2001) and a slightly more developed contribution from Visser (2012). Ackers (2015) calls for union organization based upon sectional interest, which could be viewed as an argument for niche organization in preference to general unionism. Despite this limited consideration of niche in the literature of industrial relations, it is possible to identify the origins of what are in this work conceptualized as 'niche unions'. Turner (1962) recognized that early unions organizing around craft restricted membership by occupational and geographical membership territories and were therefore relatively 'closed'. With the development of national unions from the middle of the nineteenth century, successful general unions from 1889 and industrial unions from the early twentieth century, the concept of 'trade' became less important (Webb and Webb, 1894, 1902, 1920; Clegg, 1979; Clegg et al, 1985). The result is a multiplicity of union forms, which, with the exception of general unions, are termed niche unions in this work because to some extent they restrict membership to a niche within the labour market.

Visser (2012, p 139) argues that 'Small unions can only survive if they represent a very specific niche in the labour market' and highlights the vulnerability of such unions, suggesting that 'the history of vanishing craft unions is a reminder that such niches may not outlive technological or political change'. While change may be a driver towards merger, it does not explain the persistence of numerous niche unions where certain relatively small unions such as the PFA, MU and WGGB (Writers' Guild of Great Britain) survive over time. Visser (2012) also suggests that niche unions may survive as part of a larger federated union, which can be related to the sectionalized structures found in larger unions practising what is conceptualized in this work as niche unionism. In contrast, Ackers (2015, p 96) argues against the radical influence of unions with concerns for organization and solidarity and calls for a conceptualization of trade unions 'as organisations of employees by company, trade (craft), industry, and ultimately profession.' (Ackers, 2015, p 97). While this could be viewed as a prescription for niche unions, it perhaps misses the point that unions inevitably represent both wider sociopolitical concerns and narrower sectional interests, and that larger unions tend to accommodate these through sectionalized structures, practising what is in this work called 'niche unionism'.

Although niche unions represent the vast majority of unions certified in Great Britain (BEIS, 2019; Certification Officer, 2019a), the literature of industrial relations does not adequately explain the concepts of niche union identity and niche unionism (Hyman, 2001; Visser, 2012; Ackers, 2015). In contrast, this discussion demonstrates that theories drawn from other intellectual areas are more helpful in explaining the significance of niche to trade unions (Dalgic and Leeuw, 1994; Hannan et al, 2003), in a number of respects: in recognizing firstly the nature of the niches which unions occupy, secondly that niches may overlap, thirdly that larger unions may service multiple niches, and finally that niche organizations may fail to survive or be forced into defensive mergers. However, the survival of niche unions and niche unionism against the trend of merger into general unions requires further explanation and will be explored in the next section.

How can niche unionism be explained?

Possible explanations for the existence of niche unions and niche unionism can be found in the literatures of social psychology and sociology. Social identity theory (SIT) is defined as a theory of group differentiation through which members can make their group or groups distinct from other groups (Ashforth and Mael, 1989; Brown, 2000). Turner and Tajfel (1986) draw a distinction between personal and social identity, with the latter being primarily drawn from group membership. For Budd (2011, p 148), 'Social identity theory starts with the premise that individuals seek a positive concept of themselves (self-esteem)'. Individuals may see themselves as members of 'in-groups' as opposed to 'out-groups' (Brown, 2000; Budd, 2011). In this respect, social identity could be derived or confirmed by union membership when unions serve individual members' needs for social identification. In explaining 'in-group' status, Budd (2011, p 148) suggests that 'the individual engages in self-enhancement by magnifying the differences between those groups the individual identifies with and those he or she does not' Similarly, Brown (2000, p 755), argues that 'a central assumption of SIT is that in-group bias is motivated by a desire to see one's group and hence oneself in a positive light'. This might be related to certain niche union members' need to maintain their status position (Lockwood, 1958) and also to explain the persistence of niche unions that represent a 'labour aristocracy' (Hobsbawm, 1964). However, the characteristics ascribed by 'in-group' membership may lead to unwarranted stereotyping and conflict can arise where multiple identities are derived from membership of different groups (Ashforth and Mael, 1989). These reservations may help to explain the difficulties unions face in mobilizing members to take industrial action (Tapia, 2013), where members may feel constrained by conflicting loyalties to their union, employer, colleagues and customers.

Self-categorization theory is a more recent development that explores the extent to which individuals define their own social group or relationship to other groups that tend to polarize around group norms (Hogg et al, 1990). Budd (2011, p 147) suggests that this 'extends social identity theory by digging deeper into the cognitive process that underlies the categorization process' and that 'the process of categorizing individuals into groups is seen as one of depersonalizing group members by thinking of them as stereotypes of the in-group or out-group characteristics'. However, as both union membership and the level of participation is largely a matter of individual choice, the extent to which union members inculcate group norms might be questioned. It may also be useful to draw a distinction between union activists, who might be more likely to accept group norms and members who may join for instrumental reasons. In contrast to social identity and self-categorization theories, which are drawn from social psychology, identity theory originates in sociology and relates to the roles and behaviour of individuals in society (Hogg et al, 1995). It is argued here that whereas the former may be related to the psychological predisposition of existing and potential union members to join or indeed not to join a particular union, the latter relates more closely to the roles they may perform, and that this might be a driver towards the persistence of occupational unions and particularly so in the case of professional associations.

Overall it is argued that theories drawn from beyond the literature of industrial relations help to inform questions of niche union identity and niche unionism. In particular, social identity theory draws attention to what the individual might gain through 'in-group' status (Turner and Tajfel, 1986;

Ashforth and Mael 1989; Brown, 2000). Self-categorization theory highlights the role of the individual and the extent of norming within the group and identity theory which explores the importance of occupational roles (Hogg et al, 1990; Hogg et al, 1995). These theories suggest that the persistence of niche unions, and the niche unionism practised by larger unions, might be explained by members' needs for recognition of their self-identity and status through affiliation to a group together with the need for societal recognition of their roles and behaviours.

Concluding discussion

This chapter highlights the importance of developing a new approach to understanding the projected identities of unions certified in Great Britain and the role of niche unionism. The process of historical development bequeathed the UK a particularly complex structure of trade unions. However, recent decades have not only seen a decline in membership and but also a concentration of around half of UK union membership into a small number of general unions (BEIS, 2019; Certification Officer, 2019a). The extent of merger activity combined with rebranding, the formation of new unions and the dissolution of established ones has significantly changed the unions' projected identities. The extant industrial relations literature provides some limited help in understanding contemporary union identities, with theories falling into two broad groups. On one hand there are the 'categorizers' that employ typologies with all the disadvantages of trying to fit dissimilar organizations into a limited number of boxes, while on the other there are those who employ more flexible frameworks which are now generally outdated and/or unsatisfactory.

This work also draws upon organization theory and recognizes that the projected identities of trade unions, in common with other organizations, can be understood through the analysis of certain observable characteristics. The existing industrial relations literature is remarkably limited in considering the significance of niche to contemporary trade union identities and this work therefore also draws on other disciplines including ecology, marketing, social identity theory and identity theory. Given these limitations to the understanding of contemporary trade union identities and the significance of niche, it is argued here that a new approach is required. Therefore the next chapter turns to introducing a multidimensional framework based upon the sources of unions' projected identities, derived from the systematic observation and analysis of their observable characteristics, which can be employed to better understand contemporary union identities and niche unionism.

TWO

A New Approach to Understanding Union Identities

How can we understand contemporary union identities?

Given the shortcomings of existing intellectual approaches in explaining union identities and niche unionism (reviewed in Chapter One), this chapter introduces a new multidimensional framework of analysis which advances the understanding of union identities and niche union identity in three important respects. Firstly, it demonstrates the complex and multifaceted construction of union identities. Secondly, it offers a far more comprehensive understanding than is provided by earlier theorizations, whether by rigid categorization or through the use of flexible frameworks. Thirdly, it provides for the recognition and understanding of niche union identities by means of identification of the sources by which niche unions identities are constructed.

The framework is based on more than ten years' research exploring the projected identities of unions certified in Great Britain. This involved the collection and analysis of data on unions' 'observable characteristics' (Albert and Whetton, 1985; Whetton, 2006; Balmer, 2008) to isolate the sources of unions' projected identities. For the purposes of this work, union identities are taken to be those identities which unions project in the public domain. The term 'niche union identity' relates to the projected identity of any union that restricts membership and is not general in character. Unions which project a niche union identity are termed 'niche unions'. In contrast, the term 'niche unionism' is applied both to niche unions and unions which serve niche memberships through sectionalized structures. While certain, mostly larger, and particularly general unions, practise niche unionism through sectionalized structures, the majority of unions certified in Great Britain by number have, by accident or design, adopted, retained or developed a clear niche union identity. It is therefore argued that to understand contemporary unions it is necessary to understand the extent to which they embrace the concept of niche unionism.

The research was limited to the projected identities of unions certified in Great Britain (Certification Officer, 2008–2019a), although in some cases, such as that of Nautilus, they operate beyond UK boundaries, and to primary source data collected between October 2008 and July 2019. Three certified unions, namely, Alliance for Finance, General Federation of Trade Unions (GFTU) and Workers Uniting together with the TUC were excluded from the research on the basis that they are federations of unions. Four unions that are certified in Northern Ireland were not included in the overall study (Certification Officer for Northern Ireland, 2019), but are briefly considered in Chapter Six, which explores geographical unions.

The primary method of data collection was the observation of union websites, on the basis that these provide the most readily accessible source of data, telling us what trade unions want to say that about themselves in the public domain. A full survey of union websites was first conducted in 2010 and then repeated in 2018. The website surveys enabled the collection of extensive data, with a standard survey document being used as a template in order to ensure systematic observation of each union's observable characteristics. There were potentially four levels of observation employed in conducting the survey. The first was scrutiny of a website's homepage and in a few cases this was all that the site comprised. The second level was achieved by accessing all relevant links given on the homepage. Where data could not be obtained from first- and second-level observations, the third level employed use of 'search' facilities where these were provided. In some cases the website gave the option of calling up other documents, providing a potential fourth level of observation for missing data. Documents were observed only if they were considered to be of any obvious use in supplying missing data. Some websites were restricted by the use of a 'members' area', although this did not generally restrict the collection of the required data, except for that on membership benefits.

The website surveys revealed the incidence of unions not having websites. Whereas the 2010 survey found that 58 unions did not have a website, representing 34.7 per cent of certified unions, by 2018 only 23 unions or 17.4 per cent did not. Not having a website shows some relation to scale, as these represented 37 per cent of the smallest 62 unions in the 2018 survey. The average membership of 20 unions not having a website for which membership data was available was 559.7, with none having a membership of over 2,000. Therefore it is considered that the surveys were as comprehensive as possible, given that all unions certified in Great Britain having websites were observed.

The website surveys were supported by other methods of data collection, including a preliminary survey of union names, a questionnaire addressed to all certified unions, and interviews with 23 key informants identified from question-naire respondents. The research also involved recording and analysis of changes in union identity in relation to mergers, rebranding, newly certified unions and dissolutions, as reported by the Certification Officer in email and website updates (Certification Officer, 2019b; for discussion of changes in union identities see Chapter Seven).

The research employs a mixed methods approach which is seen as having an affinity to pragmatism (Teddlie and

Tashakkori, 2011). The epistemological approach adopted is one of realism (Robson, 2002; Ackroyd, 2011; Bryman and Bell, 2011), together with reflexivity (Alvesson and Karreman, 2011) and empirical pragmatism (Hartsthorne, 1980). The researcher's ontological position is one of 'objective partisanship' (Darlington and Dobson, 2013).

Data collection involved systematic observation of the following observable characteristics:

- union names, straplines and logos;
- any restrictions to membership;
- membership benefits offered;
- affiliations and political funds.

While names, straplines and logos provide the most visible symbols of union identity, it was frequently necessary to dig deeper into websites to establish what restrictions to membership were in place in order to confirm unions' membership territories. Even where a union had a name which clearly suggested who they might represent, they sometimes only gave the initials on their homepage, perhaps missing an opportunity to make their identity absolutely clear from the outset to any potential members viewing their website. Observation of membership benefits being offered was considered to be important to identity where these were tailored to a niche membership. However, information as to whether unions were affiliated to the TUC, Labour Party or held political funds was frequently so well hidden on union websites that they might be considered to make little or no contribution to a union's projected identity.

Comparing the most visible characteristics of union identity observed in the 2010 and 2018 website surveys (see Table 2.1), it is clear that while the use of logos was similar, unions are now less likely to give their full name or initials but more likely to reinforce their identity with a strapline.

The process of analysis developed through various phases of the research and involved coding primary source data on

Table 2.1: Most visible characteristics of unions' projected identities

Characteristics observed	2010 (*N* = 109) %	2018 (*N* = 106) %
Full name	80.7	76.4
Initials	70.6	67.0
Logo	90.8	89.6
Strapline	58.7	69.0

Source: Website surveys (2010; 2018).

observable characteristics (see Figure 2.1). The sources of union identity were derived both deductively from the extant industrial relations literature (Webb and Webb, 1894, 1902, 1920; Turner, 1962; Hughes, 1967; Clegg, 1979) and inductively through reflexive analysis and pragmatic interpretation of the data. The process of coding confirmed that the primary sources of union identity – that is, general, occupational, industrial, organizational and geographical – could be successfully employed in analysing the projected identities of all unions certified in Great Britain and that many unions drew upon multiple sources. However, it became clear that further sources of union identity were needed to fully understand the complex identities projected by some niche unions. Therefore, two further groups of terms were included to enhance the multidimensional framework. Whereas 'secondary sources' help clarify unions' membership territories beyond that indicated by their primary sources, 'additional sources' reflect significant components of union identity which are unrelated to membership territories.

Comparing the primary sources of union identity observed in the 2010 and 2018 website surveys reveals that while the figures for industrial, organizational and geographical identities are broadly similar, the increase in general union identity and reduction in occupational identity require some explanation (see Table 2.2). The increase in general union identity is partially accounted for by the formation of a number of new minor general unions, such as the EFWU (Equality for

Figure 2.1: The development of coding of sources of union identity

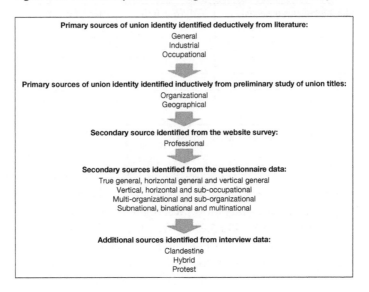

Primary sources of union identity identified deductively from literature:
General
Industrial
Occupational

Primary sources of union identity identified inductively from preliminary study of union titles:
Organizational
Geographical

Secondary source identified from the website survey:
Professional

Secondary sources identified from the questionnaire data:
True general, horizontal general and vertical general
Vertical, horizontal and sub-occupational
Multi-organizational and sub-organizational
Subnational, binational and multinational

Additional sources identified from interview data:
Clandestine
Hybrid
Protest

Workers Union), ESOSTU (European SOS Trade Union), IWUGB, PTSC and UVW (United Voices of the World). In addition, some former staff associations have adopted a general identity in order to recruit more widely, as exemplified by the former Lloyds Trade Union (LTU), which is now generally known as Affinity. In contrast, the reduction in occupational identity may be accounted for by transfers of engagements by unions to general and industrial unions such those of APFO (Association of Principal Fire Officers), BECTU (Broadcasting, Entertainment, Cinematograph and Theatre Union) and NACO (National Association of Co-operative Officials).

Overall, it is argued that the recognition of the sources of union identity and the development of the multidimensional framework of analysis introduced and operationalized in the next section provide a robust system of analysis, both for the understanding of contemporary certified union identities in general and of niche union identities in particular. It is

Table 2.2: Sources of union identity observed in website surveys

Union identity	2010 (N = 109) %	2018 (N = 106) %
General	10.1	16.0
Industrial	77.1	77.3
Occupational	76.1	65.1
Organizational	11.0	11.3
Geographical	9.1	10.7

Source: Website surveys (2010; 2018).

recognized, following Blackburn (1967), that some sources are absolute concepts while others may be variable in application (see discussion on operationalizing the multidimensional framework later in this chapter). Given that unions operate in a dynamic situation, it is acknowledged that these sources may not be exhaustive and that the framework may need to be revised to accommodate future developments. It is also recognized that other sources may be needed to understand the identities projected by unions in certain other countries (see further discussion in Chapter Eight).

Introducing the multidimensional framework

The multidimensional framework was constructed by plotting the sources of union identity which emerged during the course of the research (see Figure 2.1) against the projected identities of individual unions. The multidimensional framework (see Table 2.3) provides an analysis of 22 unions selected as being broadly representative of the entire sample. These provide at least one or more examples of unions drawing upon each source of identity. While the sources of identity are broadly grouped as general, industrial/occupational, organizational, geographical and additional, it should be noted that in some cases a union's identity is understood by sources drawn from more than one broad grouping. These unions are also used

Table 2.3: A multidimensional framework

Union	True general	Horizontal general	Vertical general	Industrial	Vertical	Occupational	Horizontal	Professional
ACB/FCS				*		*		*
Advance								
AEP				*		*		*
ASCL				*		*	*	*
BADN				*		*		*
BPA						*		*
FOA				*	*	*		
GMB	*							
IWUGB	*							
NARS				*		*	*	
Nautilus				*		*		
NEU				*	*	*		*
NGSU				*				
NSEAD				*		*		*
NUJ				*		*		
PFA				*		*	*	
Prospect		*						
SSTA				*		*		*
Unison			*					
Unite	*							
Voice				*	*	*		
WGGB				*		*	*	

Sub-occupational	Multi-organizational	Organizational	Sub-organizational	Subnational	Binational	Multinational	Hybrid	Protest	Clandestine
							*		
		*							
									*
			*						
								*	
						*			
	*								
*									
					*				
*			*						
								*	

as examples of union identities in the following discussion, although other unions are included where they are considered to be useful in informing the analysis.

To fully understand the multidimensional framework, it is necessary to recognize the significance of each source of union identity. The term 'true general' describes general unions which accept virtually any type of worker into membership such as GMB, IWUGB and Unite. In contrast, the term 'niche general' is applied to general unions which have adopted some niche characteristics, by organizing vertically, as in the case of Unison, or horizontally, as is the practice of Prospect (see further discussion of general unions in Chapter Three). Operationalizing the multidimensional framework demonstrates that beyond the general unions the vast majority of unions certified in Great Britain project a niche union identity. These unions are deemed to be niche unions because they restrict membership by one or more of the primary sources of union identity: industry, occupation, organization or geography.

The 2018 survey revealed a significant overlap between occupational and industrial union identities, with 69 unions (65.1 per cent) projecting both compared to just 13 (12.3 per cent) projecting only an industrial identity. Occupational unions were considered as such because their members do a job that is viewed as an occupation, with examples including dental nurse (British Association of Dental Nurses – BADN), musician (MU) or professional footballer (PFA). In contrast, industrial unions are such because they restrict membership to a particular industry. However, all occupational unions were observed to restrict membership, either to a particular industry or to closely related industries, and were therefore considered to project occupational/industrial identities. In contrast, those unions projecting an industrial identity such as PCS, RMT and TSSA had more diffused membership territories. Where unions such as NSEAD (National Society for Education in Art and Design) and SSTA (Scottish Secondary Teachers' Association) recruit an identifiable group within an occupation or profession, this is termed 'sub-occupational' (see further discussion of occupational/industrial unions in Chapter Four).

Professional identity was included as a secondary source of identity because it was recognized that while all professions are occupations, not all occupations are professions. Professional unions such as the Association of Educational Psychologists (AEP) and BADN were classified as such because they were observed to display some combination of certain observable characteristics, such as requiring professional qualification for full membership and demonstrating concern over professional issues and standards. These characteristics distinguished them from occupational unions such as PFA and WGGB, whose members might consider themselves to be professionals rather than amateurs. A professional identity was observed to be projected by 31 (29.2 per cent) unions, representing 44.9 per cent of unions projecting an occupational identity (see further discussion of professional unions in Chapter Four).

The term 'horizontal' was applied to unions which organize horizontally across the labour market, such as ASCL (Association of School and College Leaders), PFA and Prospect, whereas 'vertical' refers to unions seeking to recruit vertically including FOA (Fire Officers Association), Unison and Voice. While the term vertical could be applied to other industrial unions and horizontal to many occupational unions, these terms are only used where they enhance the understanding of a union's identity. This is demonstrated by ASCL, which recruits senior staff horizontally in the education sector, while NEU (National Education Union) recruits vertically, resulting in an area of overlap and competition. Similarly, FOA, by organizing vertically, is in competition with all other fire service unions.

While some organizational unions seek to represent all employees within an organization, albeit they may be constrained by the existence of another union or unions as in the case of Advance, others such as NGSU (Nationwide Group Staff Union) organize either a group of organizations or, as with BPA (Boots Pharmacists' Association), an occupational subgroup within an organization. It was recognized that some organizational unions have expanded their membership territories beyond those of the organization in which they originated. For example, Accord traces its history to the Halifax Building Society Staff Association, but now organizes in Lloyds Banking Group, TSB, MBNA, Equitable Life and Sainsbury's Bank. The main drivers to this are the trends of merger, demerger, disposal and acquisition in the finance industry. In the case of Accord, Halifax is now a bank operated by Bank of Scotland, a wholly owned subsidiary of Lloyds Banking Group, while its current incarnation is the result of the demerger of Lloyds TSB. This serves to illustrate the problems for organizational unions in responding to the complexities of restructuring in the banking and finance industry and the motivation for some to become multi-organizational unions (see further discussion in Chapter Five).

The geographical unions were deemed to be so because their membership territories include geographical boundaries other than those of either Great Britain or the UK. Six unions were observed to be 'subnational', being based in the constituent nations of the UK, three 'binational', operating in the UK and Republic of Ireland and two 'multinational', because they aspire to organize globally. The NUJ (National Union of Journalists) might be considered a multinational union, given that it has branches and members located beyond the two nation states in which it is certified. However, it is deemed to be binational on the basis that members who are organized beyond the national borders of the UK and the Republic of Ireland tend to be either nationals of one of the home countries working abroad or employees of news organizations based in one of them. NUJ also lacks the intention to become multinational, contrasting sharply with both IWW (Industrial Workers of the World) and Nautilus (see further discussion of geographical unions in Chapter Six).

Turning to the 'additional sources' of union identity, the concept of 'protest' union identity is exemplified by six unions that typically have displayed an antipathy to any form of militancy or political affiliation. All organize in competitive sectors, with FRSA (Fire and Rescue Services Association) and FOA competing with the FBU in fire and rescue, IFNS (Independent Federation of Nursing in Scotland) competing with the RCN (Royal College of Nursing) in Scotland, ISU being a breakaway union in the immigration service, UIU (United and Independent Union) being a general union and Voice competing with all other education sector unions. In each case it was observed that being a protest union was an essential characteristic of their identities and was used to differentiate them from their competitors. It was anticipated that some unions might project a militant union identity. However, militancy, which was Blackburn's (1967) third element, was not observed as a source of any union's projected identity and was not therefore included in the multidimensional framework of analysis. This is not to say that certain unions are not perceived to be militant, but rather it was not observed to part of their projected identities. Similarly, with TUC and Labour Party affiliation, which were Blackburn's (1967), sixth and seventh elements, it was protest unions that were most likely to mention not being affiliated on their websites, whereas unions with either or both affiliations gave little prominence to these.

The term 'hybrid' is applied to unions which outsource industrial relations functions and/or hold joint membership agreements with another union or professional association. This was exemplified by BAOT (British Association of Occupational Therapists Limited) and 'Managers in Partnership', both of which have outsourced industrial relations functions to Unison. Similarly, ACB/FCS (Association for Clinical Biochemistry and Laboratory Medicine/Federation of Clinical Scientists) outsources its industrial relations functions to CSP (Chartered Society of Physiotherapists). ASCL has arrangements to provide services to organizations including the Girls' Schools Association, Headmasters' and Headmistresses' Conference and School Leaders Scotland, none of which are certified unions.

In communications with both BAOT and BADN it became clear that despite being certified unions, neither wanted to be perceived as such, preferring to present their organizations as professional associations. This led to a recognition of 'clandestine' as the third additional source of union identity, echoing Blackburn's (1967) fourth element, which considered whether an organization declared itself to be a trade union.

Having considered the construction of the multidimensional framework of analysis and the sources of union identity, the next section focuses upon operationalizing it.

Operationalizing the multidimensional framework

The multidimensional framework is applied selectively to the understanding of individual unions. In some cases this is straightforward, as in the case of Advance, which is simply an 'organizational' union, because it only organizes staff within Santander Bank. However, many union identities are complex, as demonstrated by SSTA, which restricts membership to Scottish secondary education teachers and is thus a 'sub-occupational/professional/occupational/industrial/subnational/geographical' niche union. This contrasts with Voice, which recruits throughout the education system and beyond professional roles but eschews militancy and political action and so is an 'occupational/industrial/protest union'. The multidimensional framework also makes it possible for some sources of identity to be applied flexibly, rather than as absolute concepts. In the case of unions drawing upon both occupational and industrial sources of identity, the question arises as to which is the most important component. The PFA was observed to be a 'horizontal/occupational/industrial' niche union, because organizing the occupation of professional football horizontally was considered more important to the organization than being part of the professional sport industry. In contrast, the FOA, is a 'vertical/industrial/occupational/protest' niche union because it recruits vertically throughout the fire service and beyond, so that industry is considered more important than occupation to the union's projected identity.

Turning to the question of niche, operationalizing the multidimensional framework reveals degrees of niche identity, which can be seen as reflecting Turner's (1962) open/closed continuum. Operationalizing the multidimensional framework led to the conclusion that there are two broad types of certified union operating in Great Britain. On one hand there are general unions, which represent around half of UK union membership (BEIS, 2019), and on the other, those representing the vast majority of unions by number, organizing workers within membership territories constrained by one or more of the primary sources of union identity. Niche unions were observed to range from those which recruit more widely within an industry (FOA and Voice), in organizations (Accord and Advance) through those organizing occupations (PFA and WGGB) to unions organizing professions (AEP and BADN). In recognizing niche union identity it is understood that individual unions tend to be in one of two situations. Firstly, there are those with relatively secure membership territories, representing an identifiable group but not generally facing competition and typically organizing professions such as AEP and BADN or other distinct occupations, as with PFA and WGGB. Secondly, there are those niche unions which are in intense inter-union competition for members, such as FOA in fire and rescue and NEU in education. Unions in the first group were generally observed to be more focused on servicing the needs of their members, whereas unions in the second group were frequently more concerned with differentiating their union from their competitors.

The education unions in particular demonstrate the efficacy of the multidimensional framework in exposing a complex pattern of overlapping niche identities which lead to fragmentation of representation and intense competition for members. The education unions differ from most other professional unions in that none are the sole body representing their profession and also in having variable requirement for professional qualifications. As some organize administrative, technical, managerial and other support staff who may not be qualified to teach, the education unions cannot be described as 'teaching unions', with some having more occupationally diffused identities (NEU, Voice) or more narrowly focused by organizing horizontally (ASCL), sub-occupationally (NSEAD) or subnationally (SSTA; see further discussion of education unions in Chapter Four).

The provision of industrial or occupational organization within the structures of certain larger industrial and general unions was seen to support the practise of niche unionism, but was found to be highly inconsistent. Observation of general unions' websites revealed that while Prospect, Unison and Unite all gave access to sectional content, GMB did not and Community showed no evidence of having any sectional organization. Similarly, looking at some of the larger industrial unions, whereas RMT and PCS gave clear links to sectional content, others including BFAWU (Bakers Food and Allied Workers Union), CWU (Communication Workers Union) and USDAW (Union of Shop Distributive and Allied Workers) did not, so that it was unclear whether they had sectionalized structures. These findings suggest that the impact of sectionalized structures in supporting niche unionism is variable, at least in terms of what unions project through their websites.

The tendency for unions to broaden their membership territories and therefore their niche identities over time as a result of changes in the labour market is exemplified by public sector unions including ACB/FCS and Unison expanding their membership territories into the private sector as a response to privatization and outsourcing. Similarly, some organizational unions such as Accord and Advance expanded their membership territories to reflect changes in the employing organization. In contrast, Affinity, the former Lloyds Trade Union, which was derecognized by Lloyds Bank in 2015, now appears to be recruiting more widely in order to position itself as a minor general union. While some unions, including ACB/FCS and WGGB, broadened their membership territories by merger to incorporate associated occupations or to recruit more widely within an industry, as is the case with NARS, others organizing a single profession, such as AEP and BADN, have not.

What's the alternative to the multidimensional framework?

The multidimensional framework as explored in the preceding section successfully resolves the problem of categorization by allowing for multiple sources of union identity to be included. However, there might be a question as to whether it is superior to the simpler 'open or closed' approach of Turner (1962). There could be an argument, following the logic of Turner (1962), for creating a 'continuum of niche' as an alternative to the complexity of the multidimensional framework. In this case unions would be placed at points between true generals as the most occupationally open and the professional unions as the most occupationally closed. While this may hold some superficial attraction, it is argued here that it would prove unsatisfactory in application in several respects.

The first problem relates to where unions were placed on the continuum in relation to the relative importance of different sources of identity. For example, Advance, which organizes vertically within one organization, is more occupationally open, as compared with NARS, which recruits horizontally across the racing industry and is therefore organizationally more open. A second problem is that this form of analysis does not include a geographical component, which is an important element in the projected identities of unions such as Nautilus, NUJ and SSTA. A third problem is that this analysis could not accommodate the additional sources of some union identities (discussed earlier in this chapter). For example, in the case of the FOA, which organizes vertically within the fire service, it is its protest union identity which most clearly differentiates it from the much larger FBU, which organizes the lower ranks horizontally. Similarly, 'hybrid' identity derives from a union's relationship with another union or professional association, as evidenced by ACB/FCS and BAOT, while 'clandestine' identity is demonstrated by unions that show reluctance to identify as such (for example, BADN and BAOT). In each case accommodating unions which display disparate sources of identity within a single continuum is problematic.

It is argued here that a continuum approach is unsatisfactory because it is not possible to understand the complexity of union identities by reference to a single dimension, where niche union identities are constructed from a multiplicity of sources. The implication for the understanding of niche union identity is that, with the exception of 'true generals', application of a multidimensional framework of analysis is required and this work therefore goes significantly beyond that of earlier writers, including Turner (1962), whose work suggests a continuum approach, Blackburn (1967), who allowed greater flexibility in exploring union character, and all writers who suggested more rigid categorizations, including Hughes (1967), Clegg (1979) and Visser (2012).

Concluding discussion

This chapter has explained how primary source research led to the construction of a multidimensional framework of analysis. The framework recognizes the construction of union identities by reference to primary, secondary and additional sources, although it is acknowledged that the framework is capable of further development. It demonstrated that the multidimensional framework can successfully be operationalized to facilitate a deeper understanding of the projected identities of unions that are not entirely general in character and the importance of niche union identity and niche unionism. It highlights the complexity of unions' projected identities and provides a far more comprehensive appreciation of these than is afforded by earlier theorizations (reviewed in Chapter One).

It is argued that the development of the multidimensional framework makes an important contribution to understanding trade unions by providing a more robust system of analysis than is offered by either a one-dimensional continuum or by strict categorization. It avoids the problem of 'pigeonholing' unions associated with categorization in favour of a more complex analysis based on the flexible application of a range of criteria, while recognizing the complex interaction of factors which may contribute to the projected identity of any particular union. In this respect the multidimensional framework is superior to strict categorizations (explored in Chapter One). In contrast to earlier flexible frameworks (considered in Chapter One), it is specifically designed to analyse unions' projected identities and is the product of up-to-date research. The framework is therefore used in all subsequent chapters to analyse union identities and to explain the significance of niche unionism. The next four chapters look in turn at unions projecting general, occupational/industrial, organizational and geographical identities. However, breaking the analysis down into four chapters should not be seen as a form of categorization, but rather as providing broad headings under which to discuss the complex range of identities projected by contemporary unions certified in Great Britain.

THREE

General Union Identity

Introducing general union identity

General unions are usually considered as such because they organize workers regardless of their industry, occupation or employing organization and only restrict membership to their geographical boundaries. However, it is argued in this chapter that within what might normally be considered as general unions there are degrees of openness and therefore the question arises, following Turner (1962), how 'open' or 'closed' they actually are. It is argued here that GMB and Unite are the only major general unions which can be considered as 'true generals', but that Unison and Prospect are 'niche generals' because they restrict membership. Unison is 'vertical/niche/general' because it restricts membership to the public sector and public services, whereas Prospect is considered to be a 'horizontal/niche/general' because it seeks to organize the higher echelons of employment across economic sectors. Given that neither Unison nor Prospect restrict membership by occupation, industry or organization, it is considered appropriate to discuss them here under the broad heading of general union identity rather than in later chapters which look specifically at niche union identity. Despite its claim to be 'The union for professionals', which forms its strapline, Prospect was not

Table 3.1: Membership of major general unions

Union	2012	2017	+/– %
GMB	613,384	614,494	+0.2
Prospect	118,617	142,486	+20.1
Unison	1,301,500	1,377,006	+5.8
Unite	1,424,303	1,310,508	–8.2

Source: Certification Returns, 2012; 2017.

classified as a professional union because, in contrast to professional unions discussed later (see Chapter Four), it was not observed to project the characteristics of professional identity, such as requiring professional qualification for full membership or concern over the development and the maintenance of professional standards.

Scale was also considered to be relevant in understanding the general unions, with four unions having a membership of over 100,000 being termed 'major generals' and a proliferation of smaller unions being called 'minor generals'. While the four major generals accounted for 51 per cent of UK certified union membership, the remaining 13 minor generals accounted for only 0.6 per cent. Some of the minor generals are remarkably small, with ten reporting fewer than 2,000 members and seven fewer than 1,000 (Certification Returns, 2017). The four major general unions have all managed to broadly maintain or improve their membership over recent years (see Table 3.1), although in the case of Prospect and Unite this can largely be attributed to merger growth.

The current incarnations of all four major general unions are the result of mergers. GMB was formed in 1982 by the merger of the General and Municipal Workers Union with an industrial/occupational union, the Amalgamated Society of Boilermakers, Shipwrights, Blacksmiths and Structural Workers. Unite was formed in 2007 by the merger of TGWU (Transport and General Workers Union) with Amicus, which was itself the product of the merger of industrial/occupational unions. Similarly, Prospect was formed in 2001 by an amalgamation of IPMS (Institution of Professionals, Managers and Specialists) and EMA (Engineers and Managers Association). Unison was formed by the 1993 amalgamation of three public sector unions: COHSE (Confederation of Health Service Employees), NALGO (National and Local Government Officers' Association) and NUPE (National Union of Public Employees). While apparently creating more coherence of representation within the public sector, much public sector membership remains outside of Unison, in unions including GMB, Prospect and Unite.

GMB and Unite trace their origins to the 'new unionism' of 1889, which paradoxically involved organizing the industrial/occupational niches of dock and gas workers, although they quickly attracted other workers to become general in character (Morton and Tate, 1979). A historic limitation to the development of general unions was the existence of other unions, with the result that their membership was to some extent limited to 'blue-collar' sectors of the labour market and often to the less skilled occupations within these. As Turner (1962, p 221) states, 'Old unions prevented them becoming truly general organisations'. By using the term 'old unions', Turner (1962) refers to craft unions which represented the 'artisans' or 'labour aristocrats' of the working class (Hobsbawm, 1964). This problem has been partially resolved through mergers, with many unions from industries as varied as banking, building, engineering and technology being absorbed into the general unions.

While it can be argued that both GMB and Unite are now far more diverse in composition, their success in organizing the upper echelons of employment must be questioned given that the majority of unions have industrial/occupational identities, and that many of these project professional identities (see Chapter Four). Prospect has to some extent resolved this problem by positioning itself as a 'horizontal/general' union representing 'engineers, scientists, managers and specialists' (Prospect, 2019). All four major general unions have developed sectionalized structures, although the extent of sectional autonomy varies considerably between them. Individual sections tend to project industrial/occupational niche characteristics which can provide a form of niche identity to potential and existing members and can also be important in helping to facilitate transfers of engagements from minor merging unions (see later discussion on mergers in this chapter and in Chapter Seven).

The trend of merger into general unions is not without criticism. Ackers (2015 p 107) suggests that workers' interests are better built on 'some shared sense of working in the same company, trade (craft), industry or profession', which can be interpreted as a preference for niche unions. As their memberships become more heterogeneous, the question arises as to how effectively they can continue to accommodate the needs of disparate groups within their sectionalized structures. In contrast to the trend towards general unions, some mergers have consolidated union identity within industrial sectors such as those which formed NEU, RMT and UCU (University and College Union). This then raises an important question regarding the pros and cons of general unionism over niche unionism, which is explored in successive chapters.

Turning to the minor general unions, while all were observed to be true generals because, in common with the major general unions, they do not restrict membership by industry, occupation or organization, none were observed to have developed sectionalized structures. Community is the largest minor general with 25,445 members, but in contrast to the major generals has suffered a substantial loss of 19.3 per cent in its membership over recent years (Certification Returns, 2012, 2017). In some respects it has more in common with the major general unions, having been formed by a merger of industrial and occupational unions and subsequently attracted further merger partners, so that it must now be considered as a general union. However, despite organizing many diverse groups, it does not appear to have developed a sectionalized structure, although it might be expected that this would become necessary if the union grew in size and complexity. The other minor general unions form a disparate group with varying aims and objectives which are explored further in the next section.

The observable characteristics of general union identity

As might be expected, the general unions were observed to project non-specific identities, although a significant number of other unions which had niche identities also did this. All 17 general unions have websites but, as with other unions, the way they projected their identity varied considerably, with 6 giving initials, 15 their full name, 15 employing a logo and 14 using a strapline.

Three of the major general unions (Unite, Unison and Prospect) have adopted 'aspirational' titles (Gall, 2007; Balmer, 2008). In sharp contrast, GMB initially adopted the somewhat lengthy title of 'General Municipal, Boilermakers and Allied Trades Union' (GMBATU), which was subsequently shortened to GMB to streamline the union's image and is now the certified name. As its name, its logo, which includes the words 'GMB@ work', and its strapline, 'experts in the world of work', give no indication as to who is expected to join, the union's identity seems unclear. However, the union reported that market research confirmed that it was generally recognized to be a trade union.

Unite's aspirational title was adopted at its formation, apparently because there was a feeling that it wanted a single word that was emphatic, active and meant something throughout the organization and beyond, in contrast to any sort of Latin word that was less clear, as was the case with Amicus. The website gives the name as part of a logo, with a billowing flag of red and white above and the words 'the union' below, but no actual strapline. The union has previously used the strapline 'Britain's biggest union', although this was dropped as membership fell and it became the UK's second biggest union after Unison.

Unison's name is not an acronym (Terry, 2000), but was the first name adopted by a UK union which expresses aspiration (Balmer, 2008), rather than indicating either its origins or who is expected to join. Unison might have remained a public sector union had it not been for government policies of privatization and outsourcing which led the union to expand its membership territories to include public services run by the private sector. The strapline 'The public service union' does serve to confirm the union's 'vertical/niche/general' identity. The Unison logo comprises the union name together with swirling ribbons in the Suffragette colours of purple, green and silver, which the union confirmed were picked to reflect the feminized nature of the union, which is more than three-quarters female (Certification Return, 2017).

Prospect reported that it consciously followed Unison in adopting an aspirational title, explaining that 'Prospect' was chosen because it included the positive elements 'pro' and 'pros' as well as the implication of looking ahead. The logo, which comprises a large 'P' with the name 'Prospect', does not indicate the union's horizontal/general niche identity. No strapline was observed in the most recent research, although it was previously using 'The union for professionals'. Loss of this was surprising because the interviewee had thought it unlikely the union would change it because it formed an important part of the union's brand recognition. Therefore, of the four major general unions, only Unison was observed to clearly project its union identity through visible characteristics.

The 13 minor general unions were observed to employ a variety of visible characteristics to project their identities (see Table 3.2). While all are at least in theory 'true generals', open to all workers, their projected identities appear to be designed to attract very different members, perhaps suggesting further evidence of niche identity. Whereas some minor general unions were observed to be primarily focused on representation (Community, EFWU, Employees United, ESOSTU, IDU [Independent Democratic Union] and PTSC) and two upon

Table 3.2: Membership and projected identities of minor general unions

Union	Membership	Commentary on observation of website
European SOS Trade Union (ESOSTU)	4	Gave name as 'European SOS' but did not state it was a trade union; information was generalized and gave no idea what it actually does
Employees United	122	Gave a strapline, 'resolution through negotiation' and stated that it is a trade union offering representation
Solidarity	204	Gave the union name and displayed the union flag together with the strapline 'together we are stronger'; the content specifically rejects the internationalism of other trade unions in favour of one big union for British workers
PTSC	217	Gave no explanation as to what the initials stand for, but does have a logo containing a strapline 'with this name we will conquer' which also appeared in Latin as 'es subiugati erunt sub hoc nomine'; the website stresses representation

Table 3.2: Membership and projected identities of minor general unions (continued)

Union	Membership	Commentary on observation of website
United and Independent Union (UIU)	319	Gave only the name United and Independent, although the subsequent content added trade union and made it clear that the union saw itself as independent and not affiliated to any political or trade union organization
Workers of England Union (WEU)	551	Gave logo including the flag of St George; content suggests it campaigns against 'cheap labour from abroad' and supports Brexit
United Voices of the World (UVW)	819	Gave the name and the strapline 'a members-led, campaigning trade union of migrant & precarious workers'
Equality for Workers Union (EFWU)	1,017	Gave the union name and three rotating straplines 'advice and information', 'representation and guidance' and 'fighting for your employment rights'
Industrial Workers of the World (IWW)	1,671	Gave the name and initials within a globe logo, but no strapline

Table 3.2: Membership and projected identities of minor general unions (continued)

Union	Membership	Commentary on observation of website
Independent Workers Union of Great Britain (IWUGB)	1,774	Gave the name as part of a logo and initials, together with the strapline 'putting workers first'; describes itself as the 'leading union for precarious workers'
Bluechip Staff Association (BSA)*	2,206	Gave only the initials and a limited strapline 'a new way' together with a representation of a paperclip as a logo
Independent Democratic Union (IDU)	6,199	Gave initials and full name, but no clear strapline
Community	25,445	Website gave the name together with the strapline 'for a better working world'

Source: Certification Returns (2017); website survey (2018).

precarious workers (IWUGB, UVW), some stated political objectives as being internationalist (IWW, UVW), nationalist (Solidarity, WEU [Workers of England Union]) or opposed to political affiliation (UIU). In the case of BSA (Bluechip Staff Association), it was considered to be a minor general union, although it was somewhat unclear who the union might appeal to given the limited content on its website. However, subsequent to data collection and analysis, the BSA transferred engagements to Community in July 2019 (see also discussion of the impact of mergers in Chapter Seven).

On the question of whether militancy or moderation should be considered as part of general union identity, the position is somewhat complex. Whereas the major general unions tend to be moderate or militant on a pragmatic or opportunistic basis (see discussion in Chapter One), the minor general unions tend to be primarily focused either upon representation or militancy. The IWUGB exemplifies what are termed 'new-generation' unions in this work, focusing their militancy on challenging precarious employment through protest and litigation rather than traditional forms of industrial action, as demonstrated in disputes with Uber and Deliveroo (Gall, 2017; Tuckman, 2018).

Merger and general union identity

The four major general unions together with Community were all formed by merger, and with the exception of Unison can now be considered as major merging unions (Undy, 2008). In contrast, Unison, although formed by the merger, has not subsequently been active in attracting transfers of engagements apart from absorbing the College of Operating Department Practitioners (CODP) more fully into the union's structure of service groups. General union identity provides certain advantages in negotiating transfers of engagements in terms of being able to accommodate minor merging unions within existing sectionalized structures and perhaps in allowing them to retain some element of niche identity. The choice of merger partner by minor merging unions may also have something to do with identity. For example, whereas the building trades union, UCATT (Union of Construction, Allied Trades and Technicians) chose to merge with Unite, the technicians' unions, BECTU and Connect, transferred engagements to Prospect. With Prospect describing itself as a union for 'scientists, technicians and managers' (Prospect, 2019), it might be seen as representing a new 'labour aristocracy' (Hobsbawm, 1964) and supplying certain status needs to the members of merging unions (see discussion in Chapter One).

The major general unions show differing levels of flexibility in negotiating transfers of engagements. GMB requires minor merging unions such as the ambulance workers union APAP

(Association of Professional Ambulance Personnel) or ceramics industry union, Unity, to join existing sections with no element of sectional autonomy beyond a 'brand identity' in membership communications. Similarly, Unite successfully attracted unions including the Staff Association of the Bank of Baroda (UK Region) (SABB) and Britannia Staff Union (BSU) to its 'Finance and Law' section and UCATT to form the backbone of its 'Construction, Allied Trades and Technicians' section. In contrast, Prospect offers much greater flexibility by giving maximum possible autonomy to minor merging unions. This is reflected in the union's organization structure in which some members are attached to constitutional sections, as exemplified by the BECTU and Connect sections, while some other members are organized into 'industrial groups'.

Although Unison has not been involved in significant merger activity since its formation, it has concluded a number of agreements with other organizations to facilitate various forms of joint working that are recognized as a 'hybrid' source of union identity. Two examples of this are the agreement with the occupational therapists union (BAOT) and 'Managers in Partnership'. The agreement with BAOT allows it to focus on professional issues while Unison supplies industrial relations services. BAOT members (excepting those employed overseas or wholly self-employed) are enrolled in Unison and have access to the full range of services. In contrast, 'Managers in Partnership', is a national branch of Unison formed with FDA to permit senior managers in the National Health Service to join a management union. These arrangements allow unions to retain something of a separate identity and enjoy more autonomy than would be experienced by either forming or joining a section within a major merging union, while gaining many of the benefits that a transfer of engagements might bring (see also Chapter Four on the education unions).

As regards the minor general unions, only Community is active as a major merging union in attracting transfers of engagements. It has absorbed both SUWBBS (Staff Union

West Bromwich Building Society) and UFS in recent years, which appear to have chosen Community as an alternative to joining other former finance sector unions in the 'Finance and Law' section of Unite. As many of the other minor generals are extremely small, it must be questioned whether they can survive in the long run or alternatively either seek a transfer of engagement or face dissolution.

If general unionism is considered to be successful it provokes a question as to whether there should be a megamerger between two or more major general unions. Further it could be argued there is no need for more than one general union, unless perhaps it was felt that some sort of dualistic or oligopolistic competition was desirable to give workers some choice of representation. If such a megamerger happened, Unite and GMB might be the best fit as they are both 'true generals' with a range of trade sections. A barrier for Unison might be its vertical niche identity, organizing throughout the public sector and public services, albeit that GMB, Prospect and Unite also have significant public sector memberships. Prospect might be the most resistant, as a megamerger would dilute its horizontal identity and also challenge the union's political neutrality which precluded an earlier merger between IPMS and MSF (Manufacturing, Science and Finance Union). While this might also be a barrier to a merger with either Unite or GMB, paradoxically it would not necessarily be so with Unison, which accommodated NALGO as a merger partner that was not politically affiliated at its formation. Given the concerns of both Unison and Prospect over loss of identity, the most obvious merger partners remain Unite and GMB, although there do not currently seem to be any moves to conclude this (see also discussion in Chapter Nine).

Membership benefits and general union identity

The five largest general unions were observed to offer a wide range of benefits to their members. Typically these included representation and legal support, together with deals and discounts offered by commercial organizations. Union interviewees suggested that while commercial benefits may not attract many members, they provided a marginal incentive to those considering joining or retaining their membership and can help to offset the cost of their subscriptions. In contrast to many of the unions considered in successive chapters, the benefits offered by general unions were not targeted at the needs of any particular industrial or occupational niche membership. Therefore, while major general unions were observed to provide comprehensive benefit packages, these did not generally contribute to union identity. However, representation was observed to be a prominent feature on several of the minor general union websites (ESOSTU, Employees United, PTSC and EFWU). Where this was observed to be the main focus of their activity, representation was seen as an important component of their projected identity and also perhaps a significant factor in attracting and retaining members seeking individual security rather than collective representation.

Affiliations, political alignment and general union identity

The five largest general unions have adopted varying positions on political alignment. Community, GMB and Unite are affiliated to both the TUC and the Labour Party and have political funds. In contrast, Unison is fully affiliated to the TUC but only partially affiliated to the Labour Party, this being the result of a historical anomaly created to accommodate NALGO when it was formed, giving the potential for members to opt in or opt out. Prospect is affiliated to the TUC but not the Labour Party, but holds a political fund in order to campaign on political issues, perhaps reflecting the aspiration of its members to be regarded as managers, technicians and professionals. However, as no general union was observed to give prominence to TUC or Labour Party affiliation, they are considered to be minor components of their projected identities.

With the exception of Community, none of the minor general unions were affiliated to either the TUC or the Labour Party. However, a number of these unions clearly have political aspirations which do form part of their union identity (IWW, Solidarity, UVW and WEU) and, as suggested earlier in this chapter, may help to define the niche they seek to occupy. The paradox here is that unions which appear to be general unions because, at least in theory, they welcome all workers into membership, may actually be appealing to those with a particular political position in favouring internationalism (IWW), nationalism (Solidarity, WEU) or supporting migrant workers (UVW).

As regards the case for class being a component of general union identity, the position is again far from straightforward. Whereas the new general unions of 1889 were significant working-class movements, the major general unions of today are far more complex, often representing employees vertically through organizations. Prospect in particular positioned itself to organize managers, professionals and technicians who may not be seen, or indeed see themselves, as working class. As regards the minor general unions, some were clearly observed to be projecting a working class identity (IWW, IWUGB, Solidarity, UVW, WEU), while others, and particularly those focused more on representation (Community, EFWU, Employees United, ESOSTU, IDU, PTSC), were not.

Concluding discussion

A number of important points come out of the discussion of general union identity. The first concerns the extent of openness, because while two major general unions, GMB and Unite, were considered to be 'true generals', Prospect and Unison were recognized as having niche characteristics. This raises an important question for this work as to whether they should be considered as general unions if they in some way restrict membership. However, as neither union restricts membership by any combination of industry, occupation or organization, it is argued here that they can be considered as general unions while recognizing certain niche characteristics. Although all the minor general unions appear to be true generals, because no restrictions to membership were observed, they tend to focus on representation, concern over precarious workers, or pursuing a political agenda of nationalism, internationalism or political independence. Therefore it seems that these unions are tailoring what they say about themselves to attract a niche membership without formally restricting membership by any of the sources of union identity. Scale was also recognized as an important factor in understanding the general unions' identities, with a small number of major general unions dominating UK trade union membership and a larger number of smaller minor general unions.

While the five largest general unions were formed by merger, four (Community, GMB, Prospect and Unite) have successfully achieved transfers of engagements from niche unions, making them more general in composition. As the major general unions have become larger and more diverse they have developed sectionalized structures which may give members some sense of niche identity and help to facilitate transfers of engagements. However, as sectional organization tends to reflect established membership territories it provokes a question as to how effective they are in organizing in new areas of the economy. Only two minor general unions gave a strong indication of being orientated towards organizing precarious workers (IWUGB and UIU), and are considered here as 'new-generation' unions, by employing alternative models of organization (see further discussion in Chapter Nine).

Although the larger general unions tend to have more sophisticated membership benefits, these are primarily concerned with recruitment and retention issues rather than in any way being tailored specifically to the needs of their members, which contrasts sharply with some of those unions discussed in later chapters. The minor general unions were less likely to offer membership benefits, with the exception of representation, which was a prominent feature of several of their projected identities. Therefore, in contrast to many niche unions discussed in successive chapters, membership benefits were not considered to be a significant component of general unions' projected identities.

While the largest five general unions are all members of the TUC, none of the smallest 12 are affiliated. This could be because TUC affiliation is a function of scale, but alternatively because some of them do not associate themselves with the mainstream of trade unionism. As regards Labour Party affiliation, while the three largest general unions are either wholly or partially affiliated to Labour, neither Prospect nor any of the minor generals were found to be so, although several of them clearly have political objectives. As regards militancy and moderation, the major general unions tend to be pragmatic or opportunist, being relatively more militant in certain sectors than in others. In contrast, the minor generals tend to be split between those which appear more moderate, frequently offering representation, and those prepared to take or support industrial action or other forms of protest.

The paradox at the heart of general unionism is that if it is thought to be the ideal form of organization, then there is no rationale for having more than one general union, unless it is to provide some form of dualistic or oligopolistic competition. The counterargument is that niche unions can better serve members working in occupational, industrial, organizational or geographical niches by better understanding and representing their needs. Similarly, the proliferation of minor general unions with limited memberships might be questioned, but conversely it can be argued that they offer greater choice, may attract different niche memberships and, as with the 'new-generation' unions, may successfully adopt alternative strategies and tactics (see further discussion in Chapter Nine).

Having considered the general unions in this chapter, the next three focus on unions projecting niche identities based upon one or more of the occupational, industrial, organizational or geographical sources of union identity.

FOUR

Industrial/Occupational Union Identity

Introducing industrial/occupational union identity

This chapter brings together the discussion of unions projecting industrial and occupational identities because it became apparent that the largest group of unions, representing 52.3 per cent of all unions observed, drew upon both sources of union identity. It was further recognized that the established categorizations of 'craft' and industrial' (Webb and Webb, 1894, 1902, 1920; Hughes, 1967; Hyman, 1975; Clegg, 1979; Visser, 2012) fail to acknowledge this relationship. Whereas some unions are more clearly focused on a distinct occupation, such the BMA (British Medical Association), MU, WGGB and PFA, others, including RMT and USDAW, represent a range of occupations within an industry. As regards the question of what is considered an industry, this can be problematic. Taking the example of musicians, who might talk about 'the music business', the MU might alternatively be seen as organizing part of the wider entertainments industry, including the unions of performers (Equity) and writers (WGGB). In the case of the MU and WGGB, it can be argued that it is occupation which forms the most important component of their niche identity, while for Equity, it is industry that more clearly defines the union identity because it represents a range of performers including singers, dancers and actors. Therefore, where unions were observed to project both occupational and industrial identities, prominence is given to that source which it was considered most clearly describes the union's identity.

This chapter also explores professional unions, which are regarded in this work as a subcategory of occupational/industrial unions, because their identities are inextricably linked to the professions of their members. The chapter explores the extent to which they use 'occupational closure' (Weber, 1991) to defend niche positions. As the professional unions represent 23.5 per cent of all unions observed, this raises an important question as to why they are not included in established categorizations. The distinguishing features of the professional unions are that they perform a dual role, acting as both trade unions and professional associations, with concern over the development and maintenance of professional standards and normally requiring professional qualification for full membership. These characteristics provide a clear distinction between professional unions and unions such as those of the footballers (PFA) or musicians (MU), where use of the term 'professional' merely implies being paid as opposed to being an amateur.

The multiplicity of education unions are given particular attention in this chapter because they project a complex selection of niche identities and are in intense competition for members. This contrasts with the majority of professional unions such as AEP or BADN, which represent discrete occupational groups and therefore face little or no competition. However, competition may occur where the membership territories of a professional union overlap with those of sub-organizational or subnational unions. This was exemplified by the pharmacists' union (PDA Union), which fought an eight-year recognition battle with the Boots Pharmacists' Association within Boots. It finally achieved recognition in 2019, with 92 per cent of Boots pharmacists voting in favour of PDA (Robinson, 2019). Similarly, in Scotland the subnational union IFNS competes with the nationally organized RCN to organize the nursing profession.

This chapter examines the trend of mergers over recent years, arguing that there is a 'direction of travel' from industrial/ occupational unions towards general unionism, with examples including the building and banking industries. In the building industry, individual occupational unions representing individual crafts first merged into an industry union (UCATT), which later transferred engagements to Unite. Similarly, two bank employee unions, the Bank Officers' Guild and Scottish Bankers Association, merged to form the National Union of Bank Employees. It later attracted transfers of engagements from company staff associations in banking and insurance to become a finance sector union, changing its name to the Banking Insurance and Finance Union and subsequently, following a further merger, to Unifi (Union for the Finance Industry). It was finally absorbed into general unionism through the amalgamation which formed Amicus, which then formed a constituent of Unite. These mergers raise an important question regarding the potential advantages or disadvantages of general unionism over industrial organization and the extent to which any niche identity provided by their industrial sections compensates for the loss of niche union identity.

This chapter also investigates the extent to which industrial/occupational unions use membership benefits to support their niche identities by tailoring benefits to the needs of their members. In particular, the benefits offered by occupational and professional unions were observed to be most likely to be tailored to their niche memberships. These benefit packages tended to include access to specialized information, journals, advice and support which would not normally be available from a general union. As regards the affiliations of industrial/ occupational unions to the TUC and Labour Party, the research exposed a mixed picture. While a broad range of industrial/ occupational unions are affiliated to the TUC, including some education and professional unions, far fewer are affiliated to the Labour Party. It was also noticeable that no professional union was affiliated to Labour and nor were there many industrial/

occupational unions holding political funds. The chapter therefore considers the relevance of Blackburn's (1967) concerns about white-collar reluctance towards TUC and Labour Party affiliation and the extent to which these affiliations or their general political position now form a significant component of industrial/occupational unions' projected identities.

The observable characteristics of industrial/occupational union identity

The niche unions explored in this chapter represent members within clearly defined industrial and/or occupational niches. The vast majority were observed to have names which gave a clear indication of their niche identity and who might be expected to join. Exceptions included Equity and Voice, although this was frequently clarified by observing their straplines and logos. All but one of the 31 professional unions observed had names which clearly stated who they organize, with the exception being PDA, although its website clarified this. In some cases the union name can be slightly misleading, as in the case of the Fire Officers Association, which seeks to represent all levels within the fire service rather than just fire officers as its name implies.

Some occupational/industrial unions were observed to project geographical identities which were indicated in their names (see Chapter Six). These included the three Scottish education unions, AHDS (Association of Headteachers and Deputies in Scotland), EIS (Educational Institute of Scotland) and SSTA, which were observed to draw part of their niche identity from focusing on the different education system operating north of the border. In contrast, the Welsh teaching union UCAC (*Undeb Cenedlaethol Athrawon Cymru* [National Association of Teachers in Wales]) was more focused on Welsh language and culture, and required anyone observing their website to choose English over Welsh. However, in the cases of the Scottish nursing union (IFNS) and the Scottish and English artists' unions, AUE (Artists Union England) and SAU (Scottish

Artists Union), the reason for adopting a geographical identity was less clear (see further discussion in Chapter Six).

Changes in union identity sometimes reflected unions broadening their membership territories, as demonstrated by NARS in the racing industry. Attempts at organization by the TGWU and a strike at Newmarket led to the creation of an employer-inspired union in 1975, initially known as the Stable Lads' Association (Miller, 2010). Although this name would now be seen as gender-specific, the term 'stable lad' was apparently applied to both male and female stable staff. The union subsequently changed its name to the gender-neutral title National Association of Stable Staff and more recently to the National Association of Racing Staff (NARS), reflecting its ambition to broaden its membership territory beyond the occupation of 'stable lad'.

Similarly, ACB/FCS was founded in 1953 as the Association for Clinical Biochemistry, but added 'and Laboratory Medicine' to reflect its broadening membership. Unlike other professional unions in the health sector it does not represent a single profession, but rather a group of closely related ones, and therefore its niche identity is more diffused. The ACB and FCS components of the organization have a complex relationship. The Federation of Clinical Scientists (FCS) is the industrial relations arm of the Association for Clinical Biochemistry and Laboratory Medicine (ACB), which is the union's certified name, although it is the ACB which acts as the professional association. Therefore, professional and industrial relations functions are more clearly separated than in other professional unions. The ACB organizes scientists and trainees working in laboratory medicine. While all members of the ACB are members of FCS, except for corporate and overseas members, not all members of the FCS are members of the ACB. This is because some medically qualified members of FCS choose to join the BMA rather than the ACB for professional purposes. Membership of the FCS is restricted to those eligible to join the ACB. Having more fluid membership territories than most professional unions allowed it to develop in piecemeal fashion, incorporating other professional associations within the broad territory of clinical science.

Amalgamations between industrial unions were also observed to lead to changes in union identities as exemplified by the mergers of AUT (Association of University Teachers) and NATFHE (National Association of Teachers in Further and Higher Education) to form UCU and ATL (Association of Teachers and Lecturers) and NUT (National Union of Teachers) to form NEU. This contrasts with transfers of engagements in which minor merging unions generally lose something of their identities in the merger process. However, they can sometimes retain something of their former identities, as evidenced by the BECTU and Connect sections formed by the merger of those unions with Prospect (see also discussion of Prospect in Chapter Three).

Professional unions were frequently observed to avoid direct mention of being a trade union in their projected identities, with 15 using the word 'association', five 'society', three 'college' in their titles and one each 'institute', 'guild' and 'federation'. Only four unions actually included the word union, with NEU and UCU in education, PDA in health and SWU (Social Workers Union) in social work. While this might be considered evidence of a clandestine union identity, in most cases it was clearly evident from their website content that these organizations were acting as trade unions. In contrast, it became clear during the research that both BADN and BAOT were extremely reticent about declaring their status as trade unions. This was seen as evidence of a 'clandestine' component to their projected identities, supporting Blackburn's (1967) concern over whether an organization declared itself as such. Although ASCL was not observed to project a hybrid identity, it has a number of joint membership agreements with organizations representing senior management teams in schools and colleges, which project 'hybrid' identities (see also discussion of Unison and BAOT in Chapter Three).

Merger and industrial/occupational union identity

While several unions projecting industrial identities have trans-ferred engagements to general unions in recent years (BECTU, Connect, UCATT, UFS, Unity), others have resisted merger (CWU, PCS, RMT, USDAW), perhaps because they have established membership territories, a relatively stable member-ship or face little or no competition. Alternatively, there may be internal resistance to merger and a desire to maintain inde-pendence (see also discussion the persistence of niche unions in Chapter Nine). In contrast, the transfers of engagements of BECTU and UCATT can be attributed to problems of cas-ualization of employment in their respective industries which make recruitment difficult. Unions primarily projecting an occupational identity were less prone to merger in general and to merger with a general union in particular (PFA and WGGB) and especially so where they organize a profession (AEP and BADN). However, some mergers may lead to consolidation within an industrial/occupational niche, as evidenced by the mergers of ATL and NUT to form NEU and WGGB with the Theatre Writers Union. The distinct occupational identities projected by most professional unions in the health sector, such as those of the doctors and dental nurses (BMA and BADN), militates against them seeking merger partners. In contrast to health sector unions organizing a single profession, ACB/FCS, by projecting a more diffused occupational identity and with broader membership territories, has accommodated transfers of engagements from professional organizations within the broad sphere of clinical science.

Education is perhaps the most competitive sector in Great Britain, with 11 unions all having overlapping membership territories and projecting a complex pattern of niche identities. Some have shown a propensity to merge in recent years, as demonstrated by the amalgamations of AUT and NATFHE to form UCU and ATL and NUT to form NEU. ATL had previously merged with the Association of College Management which formed the backbone of a section known as AMiE (Association of Managers in Education). AMiE organizes members of senior management teams in schools, colleges and universities and can be therefore be regarded as a horizontal subsection within a 'vertical/professional/occupational/industrial' union. AMiE is in direct competition for members with ASCL, AHDS, NAHT (National Association of Head Teachers), which are all horizontal unions, representing senior management teams, and Voice, which organizes vertically through the sector. Voice, when known as the Professional Association of Teachers, had absorbed two smaller unions, the Professional Association of Nursery Nurses and Professionals Allied to Teaching. While both initially became sections, they were subsequently absorbed into the main body of the union. NSEAD was formed by merger earlier in its history and later absorbed A4, formerly the Association of Advisers and Inspectors of Art and Design. A4 retains something of an independent identity through a separate area on the NSEAD website but does form a constitutional section, a situation similar to that of the ambulance personnel (APAP) in GMB (discussed in Chapter Three). The second largest education union, NASUWT (National Association of Schoolmasters and Union of Women Teachers), was formed by the merger in 1976 of the two gender-specific unions, the National Association of Schoolmasters (NAS) and the Union of Women Teachers (UWT). However, it shows no recent indication of entering into further mergers and so the sector remains highly competitive with significant scope for further mergers.

Fire and rescue is another competitive sector within which multiple unions compete for members. FBU is the largest union and organizes the lower ranks of the fire service horizontally; it competes with the FOA, FRSA and Prospect. The FOA seeks to organize all ranks vertically through the fire service and had abortive merger talks with the RFU (Retained Firefighters Union). However, RFU changed its name to the Fire and Rescue Services Association in 2018 and also now appears be recruiting vertically through the service, making no mention of retained firefighters on its website. Both FOA and FRSA are protest unions, declaring antipathy to political affiliation on their websites and making a merger with FBU unlikely. The transfer of engagements of the fire officers' union APFO to Prospect in 2018 has not helped to streamline representation within this sector, ensuring that representation remains fragmented and competitive for the foreseeable future.

Despite the tendency of certain industrial unions to transfer engagements to general unions, many occupational/industrial unions are relatively resistant to merger and generally demonstrate a higher degree of resistance where occupation is the more important component of their identity. This can be more easily explained where unions occupy relatively discrete occupational niches, but harder to understand in more competitive sectors such as education or fire and rescue, where there is more opportunity for consolidation. While there was some evidence of consolidation by unions projecting an industrial/occupational identity (NEU, NSEAD, UCU, WGGB), it seems that despite the trend merger towards general unionism in recent decades, the survival of industrial and occupational niche unions needs further explanation (see also discussion of the persistence of niche unions in Chapter Nine).

Membership benefits and industrial/occupational union identity

Most industrial/occupational unions were observed to have well-developed benefits packages designed to meet the needs of their niche memberships and, where occupation was the most important source of union identity, these were typically more closely tailored to members' needs. This contrasted strongly with the major general unions, which although having comprehensive benefit packages, showed little or no relation to occupational or industrial niches. Whereas the benefits offered by major general unions tended to comprise discounts on goods and services which perhaps helped to attract and retain members, they were not seen to contribute to their projected identities. In contrast, where the benefit packages of industrial/occupational unions' are tailored to the needs of niche memberships, it is argued here that they should be recognized as an important component of niche identity, clearly differentiating them from general unions.

While it was observed that smaller industrial/occupational unions, in common with minor general unions, tended to offer limited provision of benefits, what was offered was frequently related to the occupations of their members. At the lower end of provision, the FOA offered few benefits beyond representation and an optional insurance package. As a protest union its main selling points seemed to be its antipathy to political affiliation, industrial action in general and the FBU in particular. Similarly, NARS offered few benefits beyond representation, together with advice and support, particularly over health issues. Many NARS members pay no subscription, a result of the union largely being funded by the racing industry as part of the trade union avoidance strategy which led to its formation (see earlier discussion in this chapter). A condition of this arrangement is that the union is obliged to give advice and representation to all racing stable staff, whether they are members or not. To contain costs and encourage membership, the union limits the provision of workplace advice and representation to non-members, whereas legal support requires full membership.

PFA and WGGB provided clear examples of occupational/industrial unions tailoring benefits closely to the needs of their members. PFA provides what is possibly the most comprehensive benefit package. Its longstanding claim of having 100 per cent membership could be considered evidence of a closed shop, but rather it can be argued that it is the result of the union having created a situation whereby membership benefits outweigh potential objections, or perhaps it is a 'social norm' (Walters, 2004). The PFA offers benefits to players including collective and individual representation, support with contractual and other legal issues together with commercial issues such as image rights. Most other benefits are focused both on supporting apprentices who do not continue in the professional game and preparing playing members for retirement. Although the union is active in collective bargaining, paradoxically most of its members are employed on individually negotiated contracts. WGGB is relatively unusual in that most members are self-employed and also work on individual contracts, although these are covered by collective agreements with the major broadcasters and producers. The union provides individual advice and representation to members over contractual issues. Both the PFA and WGGB organize their members' pension schemes and run annual award ceremonies to recognize their members' achievements. In both cases membership benefits provide an important component of their projected identities.

Competition for members between the 11 education unions perhaps ensures that benefits are important in attracting and retaining members. In some cases benefits were observed to be closely related to the occupational niche they organize (AHDS, ASCL, NAHT, NSEAD). All but three education unions (SSTA, UCAC, Voice) were observed to support CPD (continuing professional development) and in some cases trainee teachers, consistent with other professional unions. A range of commercial benefits were observed to be offered by all but three education unions (NAHT, NSEAD and UCAC). Those unions organizing smaller occupational niches were observed to offer benefits more closely tailored to their membership, as evidenced by three horizontal unions offering advice and support to members in their roles as senior managers (AHDS, ASCL and NAHT). Similarly, NSEAD as a sub-occupational union was observed to offer benefits largely focused upon the teaching of art and design.

As regards other professional unions, a further 21 unions were observed and it was again evident that membership benefits were typically tailored to the needs of their members and reinforced their professional niche union identities. These unions typically offered specialized information, advice and support together with legal advice, CPD, professional indemnity insurance and a professional journal. Some, such as AEP, advertise jobs and thus provide a marketplace for the profession. However, only seven of these unions, all in the health sector, were observed to offer commercial benefits. While no professional union could be described as a closed shop, it might be concluded that it would be significantly harder to practise their professions if they were not a member, given the extensive range of professional benefits the unions offer.

The observations of industrial/occupational unions support the contention that niche unions use benefits to maintain their niche identity. Whereas some occupational/industrial unions whose members work on individual contracts offer benefits closely related to their members' occupation (WGGB, PFA), some industrial/occupational unions offer benefits with a more limited association to their niche identities(FOA, NARS). Most education unions were observed to have well-developed benefit packages which, although largely focused on the profession, may also be an attempt to attract and retain members in this competitive sector. Professional unions, and particularly those representing discrete occupational identities, were frequently observed to offer sophisticated benefit packages, typically including provisions for professional indemnity and CPD and less likely to offer commercial benefits.

Affiliations, political alignment and industrial/occupational union identity

Thirty-six industrial/occupational unions were observed to be affiliated to the TUC (TUC, 2019), representing 61 per cent of all affiliates. This comprised 13 unions, primarily projecting an industrial identity, including BFAWU, CWU, Nautilus, RMT, TSSA and USDAW, and 23 primarily projecting an occupational identity, as exemplified by ASLEF (Associated Society of Locomotive Engineers and Firemen), MU, NUJ, PFA, RCM (Royal College of Midwives) and WGGB. There are some notable absentees, including the influential health unions RCN and BMA, although 15 professional unions are affiliated, representing more than a quarter (25.4 per cent) of all affiliates. With the exception of BALPA (British Air Line Pilots Association), the TUC-affiliated professional unions all organize in health or education. In addition, SSTA is affiliated to the Scottish TUC while unions considered to have a protest union identity were observed not to be TUC-affiliated (FOA, FRSA and Voice). Given the strong representation of professional and other non-manual unions among the ranks of the TUC, it can now be argued that Blackburn's (1967, p 38) 'white-collar' concerns over TUC affiliation might now be discounted.

Although 17 of 21 unions holding political funds (Certification Officer, 2019a) were observed to project an industrial/occupational identity, only eight of these are affiliated to the Labour Party (Labour Party, 2019). The majority of these project identities that are primarily focused upon industry (BFAWU, CWU, FBU, NUM, TSSA, USDAW), with only two being primarily focused upon occupation (ASLEF, MU). Notably, some industrial/occupational unions which are no strangers to political activity choose not to be affiliated (PCS, RMT), while certain protest unions made not being politically affiliated an important component of their identity (FOA, Voice). BADN was also observed to project an overtly non-political position but was not considered to be a protest union because unlike FOA, FRSA and Voice it is not in competition with other unions and does not therefore present itself as a benign alternative.

While no professional union is affiliated to the Labour Party, this does not mean that they necessarily avoid political activity, with five – EIS, NASUWT, NUT (now part of NEU), SOR (Society of Radiographers) and UCU – holding political funds. Virtually all professional unions were observed to be active in seeking political influence as pressure groups and involved in lobbying on behalf of their profession, irrespective of whether they held a political fund. Therefore, Labour Party affiliation might now be seen as just one of several possible indicators of a union's political position, whereas in earlier times it might have been assumed to be synonymous with it. Although Blackburn (1967) again raised the issue of white-collar reluctance, in this case to Labour Party affiliation, it might now be argued that the question is rather more about political position than affiliation. At one extreme protest unions such as FOA, FRSA and Voice make a point of actively stating non-affiliation or indeed any form of political activity, while at the other, more politically active unions such as PCS and RMT choose a position beyond party constraints. However, it could be argued that despite the protestations of political neutrality by protest unions, in representing organized labour they are inevitably political actors.

Concluding discussion

It was recognized at an early stage in the research that unions projecting some combination of industrial and occupational identities represented the largest group of unions by number of all unions observed. While existing categorizations recognize 'craft' and 'industry' (Webb and Webb, 1894, 1902, 1920; Hughes, 1967; Hyman, 1975; Clegg, 1979), this approach is problematic because it lacks the flexibility to recognize that the majority of unions draw upon multiple sources, and potentially in different measure. The research identifies a 'direction of travel' in which a number of unions drawing predominantly upon the industrial source of identity merge with general unions. In contrast, occupational unions were more likely to resist this trend, although sometimes engaging in merger activity to achieve consolidation within an occupational/industrial niche (see further discussion in Chapter Seven).

The professional unions are regarded here as a subcategory of occupational/industrial unions because they are observed to project certain characteristics, distinguishing them from other unions whose members may see themselves as professionals as opposed to being amateurs. However, the professional unions, which represent almost a quarter of UK certified unions (23.5 per cent), are not generally recognized in established categorizations. Whereas most professional unions represent a single occupation, the multiplicity of unions operating in the education sector unions received special attention in this chapter because of their overlapping membership territories that make intense competition inevitable. While some merger activity led to consolidation within the education sector, the work highlights the possibility of further mergers in both fire and education, to reduce competition and improve representation.

Membership benefits were frequently observed to be aligned to members' needs and particularly so in occupational and professional unions. In these unions benefits frequently form an important part of the union's identity. However, where unions compete for members there is more tendency to offer commercial benefits, although these are not considered to be part of unions' identities. As might be expected, smaller unions generally offered less well-developed benefit packages, frequently offering little beyond representation.

A clear difference was observed between TUC and Labour Party affiliation, with a broad range of industrial/occupational unions being affiliated to the TUC and some with substantial white-collar memberships, challenging Blackburn's (1967) idea of white-collar reluctance. In contrast, only eight industrial/ occupational unions are affiliated to the Labour Party with the majority of these having a stronger industrial identity and with affiliates being more likely to represent manual rather than non-manual workers, perhaps supporting Blackburn's (1967) concern over white-collar reluctance.

Overall this work demonstrates that the industrial/occupational unions comprise a diverse group, ranging from those professional and occupational unions with tight membership boundaries which Turner (1962) would recognize as relatively more 'closed', to unions which, if not entirely open, organize various occupations within an industry. In general, these unions are characterized by a greater emphasis on industry or occupation, by how they restrict membership, the benefits they offer or the political position they adopt. However, the implicit problem with 'closed' is that it may close out potential members who lie outside of a union's industrial/occupational niche. In contrast to general unions which can potentially recruit any worker, the industrial/organizational unions are constrained by their membership territories unless they expand these to recruit more widely or absorb other unions. This then raises a question as to how these unions might contribute more to organizing the unorganized beyond their established membership territories (see further discussions in Chapter Nine).

FIVE

Organizational Union Identity

Introducing organizational union identity

This chapter explores the niche identities projected by unions that organise within membership territories defined by a single, or closely linked group of employers. What distinguishes them from all other unions is that their membership territories are determined not by industry, occupation or geography, but primarily by those of their members' employers. The 12 organizational unions observed in the 2018 website survey had an average membership of 6,876, representing only 1.2 per cent of the membership of unions observed. Nonetheless, it is argued here that organizational unions project a distinct source of niche union identity that is not generally recognized in existing categorizations or frameworks.

While organizational unions were often formed with employer encouragement as part of a trade union avoidance strategy, they have frequently progressed to become certified trade unions, and sometimes to merge with more broadly based unions. This suggests a 'direction of travel' in which unions progress to a point where they need to show independence from the employer, achieve certification and are finally absorbed into mainstream trade unionism. In such cases the formation of organizational unions as a trade union avoidance

Table 5.1: Analysis of organizational unions

Sub-organizational	Organizational	Multi-organizational
Boots Pharmacists' Association (BPA)	Advance	Accord
British Association of Journalists (BAJ)	Palm Paper Staff Association (PPSA)	Affinity
Curry's Supply Chain Staff Association (CSCSA)	Society of Union Employees (Unison)	Aegis
Skyshare		Professional Pilots Union (PPU)
		Nationwide Group Staff Union (NGSU)

Source: Website survey (2018).

strategy can be seen ultimately to have failed. Perhaps because of this, many employers now turn to more sophisticated internal communication strategies, as represented 'in-house' manifestations of employee voice (Boxall and Purcell, 2008; Marchington and Wilkinson, 2012). However, it may be that there are still in-house staff associations with the potential to achieve certification and bring their members into the mainstream of trade unionism.

Organizational unions fall into three categories, namely organizational, sub-organizational and multi-organizational (see Table 5.1). Whereas some organizational unions such as the NGSU operate at group level, Advance and PPSA (Palm Paper Staff Association) organize a single employer, while BPA and CSCSA (Currys Supply Chain Staff Association) are focused upon an occupational subgroup within an organization. Where sub-organizational unions such as BPA, or Skyshare represent an occupational group, they are seen to project a professional/occupational/sub-organizational niche union identity. However, even where a union seeks to organize a whole institution, representation may be shared where mergers and takeovers extend their membership territories, as in the case of Advance which represents staff in Santander

Bank UK, while some former Alliance and Leicester Building Society staff are represented by CWU.

Some organizational unions were observed to project more diluted niche identities. In the case of Accord, which originated as the Halifax Building Society Staff Association, this is the result of restructuring in the banking and finance industry. It now represents staff in a group of organizations which were formerly part of the Lloyds TSB group, but in some cases are now independent entities. Therefore it now seems to be moving from a multi-organizational to an industrial identity. Similarly, Aegis, which was originally formed as the in-house staff association for Aegon employees, broadened its membership territories to accommodate members transferred to other companies as a result their work being outsourced. It subsequently accepted a transfer of engagements from YISA (Yorkshire Independent Staff Association) and also seems to be repositioning itself to project an industrial identity. Affinity, the former Lloyd's Trade Union now appears to be recruiting more widely having been derecognized by Lloyds Bank in 2015. Finally, PPU (Professional Pilots Union), while primarily focused on organizing flight crew at Virgin Atlantic Airways, also appears to accept flight crew from other airlines. This trend of dilution can be interpreted as an attempt to secure a union's future beyond the vulnerability of being tied to membership territories determined by an employer and perhaps to avoid the prospect of either dissolution or transferring engagements to another union.

The observable characteristics of organizational union identity

The organizational unions were observed to display two distinct trends in terms of their projected identities. Four had names based upon the institution or institutions within which they seek to organize, namely, the NGSU, PPSA, BPA and CSCSA. Similarly, the Society of Union Employees (SUE [Unison]) includes the employer's name in brackets while Aegis' name alludes to Aegon, the company within which it was formed. In contrast, Accord, Advance and Affinity adopted names which imply aspiration rather than organizational identity while Skyshare's name alludes more to the industry. The BPA includes both the occupation and employer. BAJ (British Association of Journalists) and PPU adopted names which refer to their members' occupation but give no indication of the institution within which they organize. The BAJ website suggests that it represents members in a 'dominant UK news-paper group', which is actually Mirror Group Newspapers. In contrast, the PPU website clearly states that it represents pilots at Virgin Atlantic Airways. Only three organizational unions were observed to adopt titles including the word 'union' while four used 'association', in three cases in conjunction with a company name. Although organizational unions that avoided using 'union' in their title might be considered to be projecting a 'clandestine' identity, it was not clear that any of these unions actively avoided description as a trade union.

The case of Advance demonstrates the changing identity of an organizational union. Formed in 1944 as the 'Abbey National Staff Association', it changed its name to the 'Abbey National Group Union' in 2002, including 'group' to reflect the changing company structure and substituting 'union' for 'asso-ciation', perhaps reflecting the union's journey from internal staff association to certified union. However, it did not change its name when it absorbed the Union for Bradford and Bingley Staff and Associated Companies following the merger of the employing organizations in 2009. The Bradford and Bingley members were accommodated within the existing structure of the union with no special provision for a sectional identity. Finally, the union changed its name to Advance following the takeover of the employer by Santander. Because Advance only organizes within Santander Bank UK rather than the parent group, it is now considered to be simply an 'organizational' niche union.

Seven unions were observed to include a strapline on their website, which can be important in clarifying who the union seeks to organize where the union name gives no indication of this. Advance employed the strapline 'Your voice at work' as part of the union logo, together with the union name and the outline shape of a group of people, perhaps indicating collective organization. While this gave no indication as to who might join, the website also carried a prominent headline, 'The only union dedicated to people in Santander Bank UK' (Advance, 2019), to clarify the union's niche identity. Although the Skyshare website did not employ a strapline, the first line of its content stated, 'Skyshare is now the recognised trade union for all pilots employed by NetJets' (Skyshare, 2019), again clarifying its membership territory. In contrast, the Accord website was not observed to carry a strapline and it was necessary to read further into the content to clarify that it was a finance sector union and which companies it organized in.

Aegis and Affinity were the least helpful in clarifying their membership territories. The Aegis website gave only 'the union' as a strapline, while the content below stated 'Aegis looks after workers' rights at work in the Finance Industry where we have a recognition agreement with the employers', giving no clear indication of who it might represent. The Affinity website was also unhelpful, with the strapline stating only that it was 'the independent trade union', perhaps reflecting its uncertain status following its derecognition by Lloyds Bank. While nine organizational unions were observed to include a logo on their websites, few contributed much to their projected identities, with many simply forming a vehicle for the union's name and/ or initials. Exceptions included Accord, which had a logo of entwined hands, perhaps suggesting the helping hands of the union; Skyshare included a pair of wings and PPU an arrow motif, both suggesting flight; and BPA had a pestle and mortar, providing the clearest association with its members' occupation.

Overall there might be two alternative motivations for organizational unions in relation to adopting an association with employers' identities. On one hand, such association might make the union seem more official, perhaps avoiding an unwanted association with mainstream trade unionism. On the other, avoiding close association with the employer might demonstrate greater independence and in the long run help unions both to recruit beyond organizational membership territories and to facilitate transfers of engagement.

Merger and organizational union identity

As suggested earlier in this chapter, many organizational unions seem to be subject to a 'direction of travel' from formation within an employing organization, through independence and certification to merger with what might be considered as mainstream trade unions. This was demonstrated over recent years by four transfers of engagements from organizational unions formed within the banking and finance sector, namely, YISA to Aegis, SUWBBS to Community, and SABB and BSU, both to Unite. In addition, NACO, which represented senior managers in the Cooperative movement was a sub-occupational/multi-organizational union, transferred engagements to the shop workers union USDAW, providing some consolidation of union organization within the retail industry.

While none of the unions observed in the most recent research showed any immediate indication of transferring engagements to any other union, the history of organizational unions does suggest that once these unions spread their wings and free themselves from the relative safety of a close relationship with the employers, that they may find themselves too small and vulnerable to continue as independent entities and that merger may become a necessity. In the case of the two small pilots' unions, PPU and Skyshare, it might be questioned what advantage lies in remaining as independent organizations rather than merging with BALPA, the broadly based flight crew union. Similarly, within the banking and finance sector, the possibility of absorption into Unite's Finance and Legal section remains a possibility for Accord, Advance, Aegis, Affinity and NGSU. The Advance interviewee recognized that while "Unite would gladly accept all the banking unions and that they would never preclude a merger but because they understood the business, were financially secure it was not under consideration".

Despite the clear direction of travel, through which many organizational unions have transferred engagements, it seems that while independence remains practical and possible, many resist merger and prefer to retain an organizational identity. However, the fortunes of an organizational union are always likely to be to some extent dependent upon those of the employer and therefore changes in ownership and struc-ture inevitably hold implications for them, as evidenced by restructuring in the banking and finance industry over recent decades.

Membership benefits and organizational union identity

The range of benefits offered by the organizational unions varied considerably, with both BPA and PPU offering profes-sional benefits, including legal support and advice consistent with that offered by professional associations and which can therefore be seen as forming a component of these unions' identifies (see discussion in Chapter Four). Similarly, the BAJ offered legal and financial support to its members. In contrast, Accord, Aegis, Advance, PPSA and NGSU offered membership discounts which may be more an incentive to join or retain membership than as a component of union identity. Neither CSCSA nor SUE were observed to offer membership benefits. Therefore it is considered that only where professional benefits are offered do membership benefits form any significant component of organizational unions' projected identities.

Affiliations, political alignment and organizational union identity

None of the organizational unions observed were affiliated to the Labour Party and nor did any hold a political fund. However, none showed any particular antipathy to political activity or political action of the type displayed by industrial/occupational unions such as FOA or Voice that were deemed to project a protest union identity (discussed in Chapter Four). Four of the organizational unions were affiliated to the TUC, namely Accord, Aegis, Advance and NGSU. In the case of the organizational unions it can be argued that following certification, TUC affiliation might be seen as the next important step in the development of these organizations as independent trade unions and may also help facilitate mergers with other affiliated unions.

Concluding discussion

This chapter recognizes that the organizational unions draw upon a distinct source of niche union identity in that their membership territories are largely defined by those of their members' employers, whether that be of a group of employers, a single employer or an occupational subgroup. It is argued here that there is a 'direction of travel' from formation within, and perhaps with the encouragement of, an employing organization, through achieving independence, certification and finally merger with an external trade union. This is evidenced by a succession of transfers of engagements from organizational unions to mainstream trade unions.

The organizational unions considered in this chapter projected very different identities, with two distinct trends emerging. While some organizational unions projected identities incorporating the employer's name within their title, others avoid any clear association the employer. As with other unions, organizational unions were frequently observed to use straplines to support their niche identities, although logos were not in most cases observed to contribute very much to their identities. In some cases, niche identity has become more diluted and particularly so in the banking and finance industry, where restructuring by the employers held implications for organizational unions. The benefits offered by organizational unions varied considerably, with two unions offering professional benefits that might be considered a component of their projected identities. No organizational unions were observed to be affiliated to the Labour Party, although four were affiliated to the TUC, which might be seen as an important step in the journey towards mainstream trade unionism and in helping to facilitate mergers.

Two important questions emerge from this consideration of organizational union identity. The first relates to the extent to which their fortunes are determined by those of the employing organization or organizations and the second concerns the recognition that organizational unions may be subject to a 'direction of travel' from formation, through independence to absorption within mainstream trade unionism. While their membership territories may seem secure in the short run, in the longer term organizational unions are vulnerable to the impact of change in employer fortunes. Although none of the unions observed in the most recent research showed any immediate indication of merging, it can be expected that further organizational unions will follow this path. Therefore it is argued here that organizational unions represent a small yet important component of union identity, which needs to be recognized. It might also be considered that given the past success of organizational unions in bringing members into the mainstream of trade unionism, albeit sometimes as an unintended consequence of employers' trade union avoidance strategies, their formation might be actively encouraged by established unions, which might ultimately be the beneficiary of any transfer of engagements (see further discussion in Chapter Nine).

SIX

Geographical Union Identity

Introducing geographical union identity

This chapter explores unions certified in Great Britain organizing within or beyond the boundaries of either Great Britain or the United Kingdom. While all the geographical unions were observed to draw upon other sources of identity, what distinguishes them from the unions discussed in preceding chapters is a geographical component to their niche identities. However, there appears to be little or no recognition of geographical union identity in existing categorizations or frameworks (see discussion in Chapter One). Recognizing a geographical source of identity is seen as important here in two respects. The first relates to the potentialities for union responses to any reconfiguration of the UK following either the secession of Scotland from the union or the reunification of Ireland. In these cases the experience of established subnational and binational unions might be instructive. The second concerns the formation of multinational unions in order to provide a more effective challenge to multinational capitalism, and in this case the establishment of Nautilus may provide a model for cross-border mergers.

The Scottish and Welsh TUCs were excluded from the analysis because they are federations rather than individual unions, on the same basis that the TUC and GFTU were excluded from the analysis of unions certified in Great Britain. Where unions such as Unite or GMB have members in the Republic of Ireland or, as with BALPA and RMT, have members routinely travelling abroad, this was not considered as contributing sufficiently to recognize them as having a geographical component to their identity. It is also acknowledged that all four unions certified in Northern Ireland project geographical identities. These comprise the Belfast Airport Police Association (BAPA), Lough Neagh Fishermen's Association (LNFA), Northern Ireland Public Service Alliance (NISPA) and Ulster Teachers Union (UTU) (Certification Officer for Northern Ireland, 2019). The Certification Officer for Northern Ireland (2019) also recognizes three Republic of Ireland unions as having members in Northern Ireland. The Irish National Teachers' Organisation (INTO) and Independent Workers Union (IWU) project 'all Ireland' geographical identities, while the Financial Services Union (FSU) organizes on both sides of the Irish border as well in Irish banks in Great Britain. In the particular context of Northern Ireland it might be considered that projecting either a 'Northern Ireland', or alternatively an 'all Ireland', geographical identity might hold political implications. To understand the identities of these unions it might be necessary to introduce a political source of identity (see further discussion of political identity in Chapter Eight).

The 14 geographical unions observed in the 2018 website survey had an average membership of 11,546, representing 2.2 per cent of the membership of all unions observed. The research identified three distinct manifestations of geographical union identity (see Table 6.1) and therefore this chapter considers the extent to which each contributes to niche identity. Firstly, there are what is termed 'subnational' unions, which relate to unions projecting an identity indicating that their membership territories are within the UK. This group comprises the Scottish and Welsh education unions (AHDS, EIS, SSTA, UCAC) the Scottish nursing union (IFNS), the

Table 6.1: Analysis of geographical unions

Subnational	Binational	Multinational
Artists' Union England (AUE)	British Orthoptic Society Trade Union (BOSTU)	Industrial Workers of the World (IWW)
Scottish Artist Union (SAU)	Financial Services Union (FSU)	Nautilus International
Association of Headteachers and Deputies in Scotland (AHDS)	National Union of Journalists (NUJ)	
Scottish Secondary Teachers' Association (SSTA)	Transport Salaried Staffs Association (TSSA)	
Educational Institute of Scotland (EIS)		
Independent Federation of Nursing in Scotland (IFNS)		
Undeb Cenedlaethol Athrawon Cymru (The National Association of the Teachers of Wales - UCAC)		
Welsh Rugby Players' Association (WRPA)		

Source: Website survey (2018).

English and Scottish artists unions (AUE, SAU) and WRPA (Welsh Rugby Players' Association). Secondly, four 'binational' unions operate in the UK and Republic of Ireland, namely, BOSTU (British Orthoptic Society Trade Union), FSU (Financial Services Union), NUJ and TSSA. Finally, two unions were deemed to be 'multinational'. Whereas Nautilus was formed by cross-border merger with an aspiration to be a multinational industrial/occupational union, the IWW represents an early attempt to form a 'true general/multinational' union (see discussion in Chapter Three).

Three unions are the subject of deeper analysis in this chapter because they were seen to be broadly representative of the three manifestations of geographical union identity. SSTA typified subnational unions operating within the UK which emphasize their geographical identity. NUJ was considered to be a binational union because it is certified in two nation states, although it also has international branches elsewhere and members working abroad. Nautilus was also initially seen as a binational union, being formed by a cross-border merger during the course of the research. However, a further merger required it to be recognized as a multinational union as it now covers the UK, Netherlands and Switzerland and aspires to bring further nationally based unions into its fold.

The SSTA was established in 1944 to represent secondary school teachers in Scotland, with the full certified name being adopted at the outset. According to the SSTA interviewee, it was formed because at that time Scottish primary school teachers were not required to have a university degree and had different salary scales to secondary teachers and it was felt that the EIS did not represent them adequately. SSTA restricts membership to those qualified to teach in secondary education and to 'transition teachers' who are 'primary qualified' and but are allowed to teach in the first or second years of secondary education. The SSTA interviewee reported that there were discussions over the years regarding broadening their membership territories, with specific requests from individuals and groups of primary teachers, but that they had resisted this. The union is therefore considered to be a 'subnational/sub-occupational/professional/ industrial' niche union. The membership territories of the EIS and AHDS overlap not only with those of the SSTA in Scotland, but also with all 'national' education unions, making this a highly competitive sector (see discussion in Chapter Four). Similarly, the Welsh teaching union UCAC competes with other nationally organized teaching unions and IFNS with the RCN in nursing. In contrast the WRPA has discrete membership territories denoted by occupation, industry and geography. However, in the case of the English and Scottish artists unions (AUE and SAU) it is unclear why a geographical component should be important to their identity and why they do not organize on a national basis.

Turning to the binational unions, the NUJ is broadly representative of the unions which organize either side of the Irish Sea. It was founded in 1907 prior to partition in both UK and the Republic of Ireland and therefore its binational identity can be attributed more to an accident of history than to intentional design. The union is constitutionally one organization with a single democratic structure. The NUJ interviewee clarified the breadth of the union's occupational coverage as including, "freelancers, casuals and staff in newspapers, news agencies, broadcasting, magazines, online book publishing and in public relations and photographers" and "some bloggers". This clarifies that the union organizes the occupation of journalism and is not necessarily restricted to print or broadcast media. Although it is considered here to be an 'binational/occupational/industrial' niche union, many members work in foreign countries for employers based in the home countries and may potentially not be citizens of either of them. Therefore, as with Nautilus, it could be considered as a multinational union; however, although firmly rooted in two countries and having members overseas, it lacks any multinational aspiration. While it is considered a geographical union because of its binational formation, the union does not project a geographical identity in the public domain, which contrasts sharply with both SSTA and Nautilus. As regards other binational unions, TSSA was formed in both Britain and Ireland before partition and remained one trade union, whereas BOSTU, although formed in 1937, also organizes in both countries. In contrast, the FSU was formed as the Irish Bank Officials' Association in 1918 and organizes in Irish banks throughout the British Isles.

The rarest source of niche identity observed in the research was that projected by the two multinational unions. Nautilus International was formed by the merger of Dutch and UK unions in 2009, with the Swiss inland navigation workers union joining in 2011. The origins of the UK union can be traced to the formation of unions including the Mercantile Marine Service Association, founded in 1857; the Marine Engineers' Association formed in 1899; the Wireless Telegraphists, established in 1912; and the Navigating and Engineer Officers' Union formed in the mid-1930s. Following a series of mergers, the National Union of Marine, Aviation and Shipping Transport Officers (NUMAST) was formed in 1985 (Nautilus, 2013). With the gradual move to two flight crew aircraft and the resulting disappearance of the flight engineer and navigator roles, the aviation side of the union went into decline and NUMAST became focused on the maritime and inland waterway sectors.

The membership territories of Nautilus are somewhat complex: as the core of the union's UK membership are merchant navy officers it might be seen as a horizontal union, but it also represents a range of other employees including harbour masters, vessel service traffic controllers, marine pilots and office staff of shipping companies. While the former Dutch union was vertically organized and open to all seafarers, the UK union was constrained by the existence of the NUS (National Union of Seamen, now part of RMT), which represents the lower ranks. Whist the line of demarcation at sea is relatively clear, the Nautilus interviewee mentioned that on land there could be more areas of overlap, as for example where shipping companies established operations on 'greenfield' sites. As many members are at sea much of the time and frequently changing ships, normal ideas of workplace organization and democratic structures are problematic. The union is organized into only three national branches, each of which holds an annual conference to which any member of that branch can submit a motion. Despite the unions' history of horizontal organization in the UK, the union is considered to be a 'multinational/industrial/occupational' union, because it is potentially open to all within the seafaring, inland navigation and associated industries.

However, the occupational component of its identity is somewhat diffused when compared to the NUJ and SSTA, where occupation was considered to be of greater significance. IWW was the only other union observed to project a multinational identity. It was founded in Chicago in 1905 (Pelling, 1976) with a multinational aspiration, but being general in character it is considered to be a 'true general/multinational union' (see discussion in Chapter Three)

The observable characteristics of geographical union identity

When comparing the projected identities of the geographical unions it became clear that whereas subnational unions tend to stress their geographical identity, binational unions generally do not and that the two multinational unions are either intentionally unclear (Nautilus) or clearly global in aspiration (IWW). The majority of geographical unions gave their full name on their website, with only three exceptions (TSSA, AHDS and EIS.) All but four unions also gave their initials on the website, all but one (Nautilus) employed a logo while all but three used a strapline, which in many cases clarified the membership territories of the union.

All eight subnational unions included the name of the country in which they operate in their titles – England, Scotland or Wales. The extent to which geographical unions embrace a subnational identity was clearly demonstrated by the Scottish education unions. SSTA uses its full name together with a logo which comprises the union's initials together with the strapline, 'Scotland's only specialist union for secondary teachers'. Both SSTA and AHDS employ the blue and white Scottish national colours. The AHDS logo is in the shape of a cartoon figure with a mortar board and body formed of the Scottish Saltire, under which it states 'representing school leaders'. Its strapline, 'AHDS is Scotland's only union dedicated to promoted teachers in primary, nursery and ASN schools', further clarifies its membership territories. While both unions clearly project a Scottish identity, the EIS website did not give the full name any prominence, nor did it provide a strapline or utilize the blue and white national colours and therefore its Scottish identity was observed to be more limited. The Welsh education union, UCAC, uses the green and white of the Welsh flag as the predominant colours on its website. As the website appears first in Welsh and then requires the observer to opt for English, it can be seen as projecting a clear subnational identity. In addition to its name, the WRPA's logo comprises a dragon wrapped around the union's initials and employs the red and white colours of the national team, again projecting a very strong geographical identity. In contrast, neither of the artists unions (AUE and SAU) include any observable characteristic suggesting a geographical identity beyond that indicated by their names. However, the IFNS incorporates a thistle motif as a logo to reinforce its Scottish identity.

While most subnational unions tended to derive a strong element of their projected identities from geographical components, only one of the binational unions gave any such indication. The exception was the BOSTU which gave its name as the 'British and Irish Orthoptic Society' on its website. The NUJ projects a 'binational/occupational/industrial' identity and BOSTU a 'binational/professional/occupational/industrial' identity, because they organize distinct occupations, whereas the FSU and TSSA, in representing a range of occupations within their industries, are seen as 'binational/industrial' unions. The NUJ retains the certified name that was adopted at its foundation, with the word 'national' being retained following the creation of the Republic of Ireland. Paradoxically, the word 'national' in the union name might otherwise imply that a union was wholly or at least primarily committed to operating in a single national state. Today the union is most commonly known by its initials, the NUJ. The union logo comprises the union initials in large font together with the full name in smaller print within a rectangle and the strapline 'winning for you at work'. However, it is the occupation of journalism which most clearly defined the union's niche identity, as there is no mention of home country in its certified name, initials, logo or strapline. The FSU website gives the full name of the union, but does not employ either a logo or strapline to clarify its membership territories and makes no mention of its binational status, despite being predominantly based in the Republic of Ireland. The TSSA homepage gives its initials, which form a logo, but does not give its full name or utilize a strapline. The nearest it comes to projecting a binational status is a link to 'TSSA Ireland'.

Turning to the multinational unions, the name of Nautilus International is derived from industry and occupation and is geographically non-specific, allowing it to accommodate further nationally based maritime unions. According to its interviewee, Nautilus was chosen because, "we needed to come up with a name that worked across both sides of the North Sea" and that was "instantly maritime in the Netherlands and in the UK". The 'International' element of the name also reflects the union's aspiration to achieve further mergers. The union utilizes a 'compass-like' logo, but there is no strapline. The Nautilus interviewee explained it had used the phrase 'uniting maritime professionals' but that with the move into Switzerland it was now the biggest union representing inland navigation workers, which made maritime references inappropriate. In contrast, the IWW, which was formed to be an international general union, projects a clear multinational identity, with a logo that includes the full name and initials over a representation of the northern hemisphere.

Merger and geographical union identity

The geographical unions display quite different propensities to merge. The SSTA reported being approached by ATL some years ago but, given their concern over the differences in the Scottish education system, it seems unlikely that they would participate in a cross-border merger. However, merger with either the much larger IES or the AHDS seems a more likely prospect given that the unions could retain a Scottish identity. The prospect of a merger involving the Welsh teaching union UCAC seems even less likely given that its overriding concern seems to be the promotion of Welsh language and identity, although in contrast to the Scottish education unions it does not face any particular differences in the education system. Similarly, there did not seem any obvious barrier to IFNS transferring engagements to RCN, beyond its national identity. However, two subnational unions from the finance industry which had a local basis of organization have transferred engagements in recent years (SUWBBS, YISA).

None of the binational unions showed any immediate inclination to merge. In the case of the NUJ and the BOSTU they represent distinct occupational groupings. The NUJ reported valuing its independence, although this had more to do with its occupational rather than its geographical identity. The NUJ interviewee explained that the leadership made survival as an independent union a priority when the union had encountered a severe financial crisis. However, it does face limited competition from two smaller unions, BAJ and IOJ (Institute of Journalists), which might at some stage become potential merger partners. BOSTU, having a dual role as a trade union and professional association, as with other professional associations, seems less likely to merge (as discussed in Chapter Four). FSU seems unlikely to merge with any other finance sector union at present given its clear identity as a union for employees of banks on the island of Ireland and Irish banks in Great Britain, although any future reorganization in the banking and finance industry may result in further restructuring of union organization (see discussion in Chapter Four). Finally, in the case of the TSSA, there might always be the possibility merger with the larger transport union, RMT, or with a general union. However, TSSA can be seen as part of a structure of union representation in the railway industry in which the train drivers' union ASLEF organizes the 'labour aristocracy' (Hobsbawm, 1964), while TSSA represents white-collar occupations and the RMT more blue-collar ones.

Whereas most geographical unions have not engaged in merger throughout their history, Nautilus was not only formed by merger, but positions itself as a major merging union with multinational aspirations. As a preparation for merger, the British and Dutch unions changed their names to 'Nautilus UK' and 'Nautilus NL' respectively. The two unions merged formally in 2009, with the Swiss union Unia joining in 2011 and then another Dutch union in 2015. Nautilus might be seen as providing a model for the formation of further multinational unions through further cross-border mergers (Gennard, 2009). However, whereas Nautilus seeks to organize a multinational industry, a potential barrier might be that many unions certified in Great Britain have significant public sector memberships, making merger across national boundaries less likely. Alternatively, it could be argued that the seemingly unassailable power of multi-national capital may make the formation of multinational unions both more likely and more desirable. Finally, in the case of IWW, merger never seemed to be an issue and therefore seems unlikely despite its small UK membership.

Membership benefits and geographical union identity

All the geographical niche unions considered in this chapter offered a range of benefits which were sometimes closely related to the industrial and/or occupational niches which they occupied, rather than having any particular geographical significance. While all geographical unions offered representation, what was offered in addition to this was highly variable. Perhaps because of the competitive situation in which they find themselves, the three subnational Scottish education unions were all observed to offer comprehensive membership benefits (see discussion of educational unions in Chapter Four). The AHDS was observed to offer access to CPD together with a range of benefits including free financial advice, a tax rebate service, insurance cover for personal accident and for loss or damage to property while on school premises. Similarly, EIS offered benefits including support for CPD, legal services, financial services and other commercial discounts. SSTA offered a more comprehensive range of benefits, with an extensive range of legal, financial and commercial benefits including a car purchase scheme. In contrast UCAC mentioned offering a range of benefits to members but asked readers to contact it for more information. As regards the other subnational unions, IFNS offered legal and insurance benefits together with a magazine, while the AUE offered free training courses, a package of insurance benefits and mentioned that free legal advice was currently being negotiated. The SAU also offers training and an online shop, but as it has a members' area it is possible that further benefits are available. The WRPA has a benevolent fund, offers a personal development programme for current players and support services for ex-players, which can be seen as similar to the type of benefits offered by the PFA (see discussion in Chapter Four).

BOSTU was the only binational union observed to project a professional identity and to offer benefits which might be seen as reinforcing this. These included publishing a professional journal and access to CPD, but as the website has a members' area it is again possible that further benefits might be accessed through this. Similarly the NUJ offers benefits including training, press passes and legal support over professional issues, which might be seen to reinforce its occupational identity. The NUJ interviewee described it as one of the "gatekeepers" of the industry in distributing press cards in the UK and the Republic of Ireland. As employers also do this it cannot be argued that the union is maintaining a closed shop, but as trainees and freelancers may not necessarily have employers, there may be some element of occupational closure. In contrast, neither FSU nor TSSA were observed to offer commercial benefits.

Turning to the multinational unions, Nautilus offers representation and legal support with particular emphasis on cases concerning certificates of competency and also commercial discounts. Nautilus is active in representing members over professional and health and safety issues. The Nautilus interviewee stated that "one of the biggest issues for seafarers these days is the concept of criminalization and the way in which they so often end up in court". Therefore it is argued here that many of the benefits which Nautilus offers are clearly related to its occupational/industrial identity rather than having any particular geographical significance. In contrast, IWW does not appear to offer any benefits beyond its own online shop selling union memorabilia.

Affiliations, political alignment and geographical union identity

The research did not reveal any particular association between the identities of geographical unions and their political alignments or affiliations. Of the 14 geographical unions, seven were affiliated to the TUC (BOSTU, NUJ, TSSA, Nautilus, EIS, UCAC, AUE) and four affiliated to the STUC (Scottish Trades Union Congress) (EIS, NUJ, SSTA, TSSA). Only one geographical union was affiliated to the Labour Party (TSSA) and only two held political funds (EIS, TSSA). Despite projecting Scottish identities, none of the Scottish unions appeared to support Scottish nationalism or to have any formal link with the Scottish National Party but rather seemed more concerned with differences between the Scottish education system and that operating south of the border. Similarly, there was no evidence of UCAC campaigning for Welsh independence or of it being affiliated to Plaid Cymru. However, the UCAC website did show evidence of participation in joint discussions at the Plaid 2014 conference (UCAC, 2019). While the union does not experience the same differences in the education system as the Scottish education unions, it seems more concerned with campaigns for the teaching of Welsh language and culture, which might be interpreted as being nationalistic.

Interestingly, while two of the binational unions were observed to be affiliated to STUC (NUJ, TSSA), only two of the subnational unions projecting a Scottish identity were (EIS, SSTA). Three binational unions (FSU, NUJ, TSSA), were affiliated to the Irish Congress of Trade Unions (ICTU). Paradoxically, BOSTU, which is the only binational union to project a geographical identity was not. The ICTU operates across the island of Ireland and reports having 44 affiliates (Irish Congress of Trade Unions, 2019). However, many of these were observed to be unions primarily based in the United Kingdom and to give their office addresses as either being located in Northern Ireland or on the mainland of Great Britain. This seems to confirm that while these unions may have a foothold in the Republic of Ireland, they should not be considered binational. As might be expected of a multinational union, Nautilus holds a broad range of affiliations both in the home countries and to international organizations. Although it does not have a political fund and is not affiliated to the Labour Party, it is affiliated to the TUC and FNV (*Federatie Nederlandse Vakbeweging* [Federation of Dutch Trade Unions]), the Netherlands trade union centre. In contrast, the IWW, while being the most overtly political multinational union, does not appear to have any particular affiliations, although it does claim to be established in a number of countries around the world.

Concluding discussion

In exploring the manifestation of geographical niche union identity it became clear that the unions considered in this chapter demonstrated quite different manifestations of geographical identity. Whereas subnational unions tend to emphasize their geographical identities, binational unions tend not to do so and multinational unions projected an international identity. Three of the Scottish unions, ADHD, IFNS and SSTA, together with the Welsh unions, UCAC and WRPA, were observed to project the strongest subnational identities, although in each case this was seen to fall short of overt support for nationalism. In the case of the Scottish education unions, projecting a subnational geographical identity seems to be more to do with differences in the education system. This was demonstrated by the SSTA which successfully differentiates itself occupationally from the both the EIS and AHDS in Scotland and geographically from the multiplicity of teaching unions operating in the UK.

In the case of two binational unions (NUJ, TSAA), their geographical identity is the result of an historical anomaly resulting from the partition of Ireland. However, the NUJ also to some extent operates on a multinational basis, with many members working outside of the home countries and in some cases attached to overseas branches. Any future secession of Scotland from the UK or reunification of Ireland would raise further issues for geographical union identity. While on the one hand, the subnational unions might be a model for unions adopting a Scottish identity, on the other, binational unions operating in the UK and Ireland provide an alternative model binational operation.

While this research found relatively limited evidence of multinational union organization, Nautilus provides a model for further cross-border mergers and the development of multi-national unions (Gennard, 2009). This in turn raises the possibility of more effective challenges to multinational capital than can be achieved by nationally based unions, which are currently reliant on achieving cooperation through international trade union organizations. However, while the multinational nature of capital may make further multinational unions an attractive alternative, a clear limitation is the significant public sector membership of many major unions certified in Great Britain. In contrast to Nautilus, other geographical unions seemed to be fairly resistant to merger, even where there was clear scope for this. In contrast, the IWW raised the possibility of an ultimately 'open' union (Turner, 1962), a 'true general/multinational', free from industrial, occupational, organizational or geographical limitations to its membership territories. Pelling (1960, p 111) states: 'Its objective was to unite the workers in one centralised organisation, without distinction of trade, skill, race or ethnic origin'. Despite these grand ambitions and more than a century later, it can now be seen that these have not been realized. This suggests that multinational industrial organization with cross-border mergers, along the lines demonstrated by Nautilus, might be a more productive route to countering the seemingly unassailable progress of multinational capitalism than the model established by the IWW.

As regards the question of why unions should adopt a geographical identity rather than being restricted to national borders, the unions considered in this chapter offer contrasting explanations. The Scottish education unions restrict their area of operation to Scotland because of differences in the education system but may also benefit from an association with a Scottish identity, if not with Scottish nationalism. In contrast, UCAC does not face the same differences in the education systems but appears more focused on the Welsh language and identity. The WRPA clearly relies on a strong geographical component to its identity in organizing the players of Wales' national sport. The binational unions, either by historical accident or by design, organize on both sides of the Irish Sea, but with the exception of BOSTU, do not to stress their binational status. It is unclear what the English and Scottish artists or Scottish nurses' unions gain from projecting a subnational component to their identity. Finally, in the case of multinationals, adopting this form of niche union identity gives Nautilus greater potential to organize a multinational industry, whereas for the IWW it embodies the ambition of being a global general union. While this investigation has established that geographical identity is currently a relatively rare source of niche union identity, it may yet become more significant, both as a response to any reconfiguration of the UK and as a challenge to multinational capitalism.

SEVEN

The Developing Story of Union Identities

Introducing the developing story of union identities

In exploring the question of union identities it was recognized from the outset that with unions' projected identities changing considerably over time, what was being observed was effectively a 'snapshot of a moving picture'. Therefore this chapter explores four key drivers towards change in union identities, namely the impact of mergers, rebranding, the formation of new unions and the dissolution of existing ones. In doing so, it aims to identify the most significant trends in the development of union identities and niche unionism.

The research recognized that union amalgamations inevitably lead to new identities as exemplified by the merger of ATL and NUT to form NEU. However, where minor merging unions transfer engagements to major merging unions there can be a loss of identity. In addition to new identities created by merger, many unions have rebranded in recent years, frequently adopting new names. While most union names have traditionally indicated the occupational or industrial membership territories of the union, many unions have now adopted 'aspirational' titles that do not clarify who might join (Gall, 2007; Balmer, 2008). In other cases, new names are adopted to broaden a union's membership territories, as seemed to be the case when the Retained Firefighters Union changed its name to the Fire and Rescue Services Association.

A number of new unions have been formed in recent years, although they tend to be small and frequently prone to failure, as evidenced by the short-lived 'Pop-Up Union' formed at the University of Sussex (Certification Officer, 2016). However, it is recognized that all existing unions originated at some point and that new unions may have the potential to grow to establish a viable membership within an unorganized area of the labour market and perhaps ultimately to merge with other unions. While negotiating a transfer of engagements is normally an option for failing unions, some simply choose to dissolve the organization, as was the case with the Retired Officers Association (ROA), and therefore dissolution is also a factor in the developing story of union identities and niche unionism.

What is the impact of mergers?

The merger process has continued over recent years, with the Certification Officer (2019b) reporting 11 unions as having transferred engagements between 4 July 2014 and 31 September 2019 (see Table 7.1). What is clear from this analysis is that with the exception of BSA, the transferor union had a narrower niche identity than the transferee union, resulting in some dilution of niche identity. In nine cases the transfer was to a general union, with the exceptions being those of NACO to USDAW, the established retail industry union and YISA to Aegis, a multi-organizational union which appears to be becoming a finance industry union. In the case of three unions representing managerial and technical staff, the transfer was to Prospect: APFO, BACM–TEAM (British Association of Colliery Management – Technical Energy and Administrative Management) and BECTU. This can be seen as consistent with Prospect projecting a 'horizontal/general' identity and seeing itself as organizing, 'professionals, managers, technical

Table 7.1: Unions transferring engagements

Transferor union	Transferee union	Change in union identity
Association of Principal Fire Officers (AFPO)	Prospect	Horizontal/occupational/industrial to horizontal/general
Bluechip Staff Association (BSA)	Community	Minor general to true general
Britannia Staff Union (BSU)	Unite	Organizational to true general
British Association of Colliery Management – Technical Energy and Administrative Management (BACM-TEAM)	Prospect	Horizontal/occupational/industrial to horizontal/general
Broadcasting Entertainment Cinematograph and Theatre Union (BECTU)	Prospect	Occupational/industrial to horizontal/general
National Association of Co-operative Officials (NACO)	USDAW	Horizontal/occupational/industrial to industrial
Staff Association of the Bank of Baroda (UK Region) (SABB)	Unite	Organizational to true general
Staff Union West Bromwich Building Society (SUWBBS)	Community	Organizational to true general
UFS	Community	Industrial to true general
Union of Construction, Allied Trades and Technicians (UCATT)	Unite	Industrial to true general
Unity	GMB.	Industrial to true general
Yorkshire Independent Staff Association (YISA)	Aegis	Organizational to multi-organizational/industrial

Source: Certification Officer (2019b); website survey (2018).

experts and craftspeople working in a huge range of industries' (Prospect, 2019; see also discussion in Chapter Three). The choice of Prospect as a merger partner by these unions in preference to a true general might be considered as being related to the identity needs of their members, who frequently occupy higher status roles within their employing organizations (see also discussions in Chapter One on identity needs and status and Chapter Nine on the persistence of niche unions).

The only amalgamation during this period was that between the ATL and NUT to form NEU in 2017. While this merger has made some progress towards greater coherence of representation in the education sector, as both transferor unions projected 'occupational/professional/industrial' identities, there was no significant impact on the industrial component of their niche identity, but loss of the words 'teacher' and 'lecturer' has perhaps diluted their occupational/professional identity.

What is the impact of rebranding?

Turning to the issue of a rebranding, a number of unions have adopted new names in recent years, often in combination with redesigned logos and straplines, and in some cases as part an active process of 'corporate identity management' (Balmer and Soenen, 1999). Some unions have followed the traditional approach of selecting a name that broadly describes the union's membership territories. This is illustrated in the education sector, where mergers have led to the formation of both UCU and NEU. In contrast, a number of unions have adopted 'aspirational' titles which may give a message about the union but give no indication as to who might join (Gall, 2007; Balmer, 2008; see discussion in Chapter One). Unison was the first UK union to adopt an aspirational title when it was formed by the amalgamation of three public sector unions in 1993 (Terry, 2000). All three merger partners had names suggesting a niche identity, namely the Confederation of Health Service Employees, the National Union of Public Employees, and the National Association of Local Government Officials. Adopting the name Unison avoided any clumsy attempt to accommodate the former union names, as was the case four years earlier when GMB initially adopted the title General Municipal, Boilermakers and Allied Trades Union. In contrast, the name Unison may perhaps represent the aspiration of the amalgamating unions coming together to work in unison. However, as with other aspirational union titles, it does not convey the union's niche identity, in this case that it is a 'vertical/general' union, organizing in the public sector and public services.

Twelve unions had names which could be described as either aspirational or at least were non-specific in terms of giving no indication of their membership territories (see Table 7.2). While most of these union names express aspiration, some are less clear. For example, Skyshare is an organizational union representing pilots and whereas the 'Sky' element more clearly suggests the airline industry, the 'share' part might perhaps be considered as relating to collective organization. Myunion did not have a website and therefore, despite its name, it was hard to ascertain who might be expected to join. Nautilus was included in this analysis because its name is relatively non-specific, although it can be perceived as suggesting seafaring, which the union's interviewee confirmed was the case (see discussion in Chapter Six).

Analysis of aspirational union titles confirms that they do not seem to have any particular relationship to the source or sources of a union's projected identity. Whereas unions such as Accord and Affinity organize in multiple institutions, Advance organizes only in the Santander Bank UK, Voice operates across the education sector while Community, Solidarity, Unite and Unison are all general unions, albeit that Unison is confined to the public sector and public services. In addition to those unions with aspirational or non-specific names (listed in Table 7.2), 11 others have a certified name based upon or including their initials, as exemplified by FDA, GMB, POA and R&C Trade Union. In these cases it might be questioned to what extent their projected identities are recognized in the public domain, both in relation who they represent and in some cases as to their being trade unions. What became clear during the research is that where unions' names give no indication of their membership territories, it is necessary to use

Table 7.2: Unions with aspirational or non-specific names

Name	Projected identity
Accord	Multi-organizational
Advance	Organizational
Affinity	Multi-organizational
Community	True general
Myunion	No website found
Nautilus International	Industrial/multinational
Prospect	Horizontal/general
Skyshare	Organizational
Solidarity	True general
Unison	Vertical/general
Unite	True general
Voice	Occupational/industrial/professional

Source: Certification Officer (2019b); website survey (2018).

other indicators such as logos, straplines and website content to fully understand their projected identities. This raises an important question concerning how potential members might know which union is the most appropriate for them to join (see further discussion in Chapter Nine).

The Certification Officer (2019b) reported five unions as having changed their names in the period from 4 July 2014 to 31 September 2019 (see Table 7.3). Interestingly, none of them chose an aspirational title, but rather each adopted one which broadly described their membership territories. In the case of both the Fire and Rescue Services Association and the National Association of Racing Staff this seemed to be because the unions were expanding their membership territories to recruit more widely within their respective industries. In contrast, in the cases of the Leeds Building Society Colleague Association (LBSCA) and College of Podiatry (COP), the unions might be looking to update their names. Finally, the Whatman International Staff Association (WISA) was dissolved in October 2015, having changed its name only the previous February. Although the reason for the change is unclear, it

Table 7.3: Unions changing names and their projected identities

Former name of union	New name of union	Projected identity
Leeds Building Society Staff Association (LBSSA)	Leeds Building Society Colleague Association (LBSCA)	No website found
National Association of Stable Staff (NASS)	National Association of Racing Staff (NARS)	Occupational/industrial
Retained Firefighters Union (RFU)	Fire and Rescue Services Association (FRSA)	Occupational/industrial
The Society of Chiropodists and Podiatrists (SCP)	The College of Podiatry (COP)	Occupational/professional/industrial
Whatman Staff Association (WSA)	Whatman International Staff Association (WISA)	No website found

Source: Certification Officer (2019b); website survey (2018).

might perhaps have been a last effort to popularize the union and/or alternatively to broaden its membership territories (see later discussion in this chapter on union dissolutions).

While rebranding frequently results from an amalgamation or a union's decision to expand its membership territories, it might be questioned what benefits are gained from the process when compared to maintaining an established identity. Whereas rebranding may provide a fresh identity that may appeal to existing and potential members, there are also costs. These may not only be financial but might involve a loss of established identity which could have an adverse effect on recruitment if potential members fail to recognize the organization as the appropriate union, or indeed as a union at all. Burghausen and Balmer (2015), discuss the concept of 'corporate heritage identity stewardship' which relates to the maintenance of past identity and its relevance to the present and future of the organization. Therefore it may be important for unions not only to consider the potential benefits of rebranding, but also the value of what they have already in terms of an established and recognized identity and how this might be maintained (see also discussion on heritage identity stewardship in Chapter One).

What is the impact of new unions?

New unions continue to be formed, with the Certification Officer (2019b) reporting 16 unions as either being listed or certified as trade unions in the period from 4 July 2014 to 31 September 2019 (see Table 7.4). While these unions were new to the certification process, it cannot be assumed that each of them was necessarily an entirely new organization, given that some may have had a significant history before seeking certification. Observation of these unions' websites revealed that four projected a general identity while ten displayed some combination of

Table 7.4: New unions listed or certified as trade unions

Name	Projected identity
Artists' Union England (AUE)	Occupational/industrial
Association of Local Council Clerks (ALCC)	Occupational/industrial
Cleaners and Allied Independent Workers Union (CAIWU)	Occupational/professional/industrial
Confederation of British Surgery (CBS)	Occupational/industrial
CU Staff Consultative Group (CUSCG)	No website found.
CWOATA Trade Union	Occupational/industrial
Welsh Local Government Association	Industrial/occupational
Driver and General Union (DGU)	Occupational/industrial
Equality for Workers Union (EFWU)	True general
European SOS Trade Union (ESOSTU)	True general
National Crime Officers Association (NCOA)	Occupational/industrial
Poole Greyhound Trainers Union (PGTU)	No website found
Psychotherapy and Counselling Union (PCU)	Occupational/industrial
PTSC	True general
R&C Trade Union (RCTU)	Occupational/industrial
United Voices of the World (UVW)	True general

Source: Certification Officer (2019b); website survey (2018).

occupational and industrial niche identities. In the case of two unions, no website could be found and as they were yet to submit their first certification return it was not possible to access any further information. However, the Poole Greyhound Trainers Union (PGTU) appears from its name to project an occupational/industrial/geographical identity, while the identity of the CU Staff Consultative Group (CUSCG) is unclear.

The potential impact of new unions is demonstrated by the IWUGB. Founded in 2012, it can be seen as representative of several 'new-generation' unions and says of itself, 'IWUGB campaigns are known for being bold, vibrant, loud and effective' (IWUGB, 2019). It has successfully employed a combination of industrial and legal action in some well-publicized cases over issues such as bogus self-employment in the 'gig economy' at Deliveroo and outsourcing at the University of London (Williams, 2017; Tuckman, 2018). IWUGB emerged from the IWW and has itself spurned two 'sister' unions, the Cleaners and Allied Independent Workers Union (CAIWU) and UVW (Gall, 2017). IWUGB has grown rapidly in membership, reporting 437 members in 2012 and 1,671 in 2017 (Certification Returns, 2012, 2017). The success of IWUGB to date might be attributed to the plight of precarious workers and the shortcomings of legal protection and enforcement, but also to the failure of some established unions to organize more effectively in unorganized sectors of the economy.

The formation of 'new-generation' unions raises a question for this work concerning whether they project a new form of identity. In relation to the multidimensional framework introduced earlier (see Chapter Two), the IWUGB and UVW are considered to be 'true general' unions, whereas the CAIWU projects an 'industrial/occupational' niche identity. What distinguishes them from most other unions is the combination of tactics which they employ to support the struggles of precarious workers. However, these tactics are, or have been, employed by other unions from time to time, as exemplified by recent campaigns run by the established BFAWU. Therefore, while these unions may represent a new generation of trade unions, successfully employing a particular combination of tactics, it is not considered that they are projecting a new source of union identity.

While new unions tend to be small in membership and prone to failure, it is argued here they bring new members into the mainstream of trade unionism and that each has the potential to grow and develop. It may be useful to recall that the roots of both GMB and Unite can be traced to the formation of the new unions in 1889 and that they were initially niche unions of gas and dock workers. These two major general unions are repositories of many former niche unions which transferred engagements to them over the years, all of which could trace their origins to the formation of new unions at some point in time. Therefore the contemporary strength of major general unions in particular, and of the trade union movement overall, can to some extent be attributed to the historic formation of new unions. Following this line of thinking, it is argued here that there is a case for encouraging and supporting the formation of new unions in areas of the labour market where established unions find it hard to organize (see discussion of union organization in Chapter Nine).

What is the impact of union dissolutions?

The final part of the story of changing union identities relates to the dissolution of established unions. In the period from 4 July 2014 to 31 September 2019 the Certification Officer (2019b) reported 16 unions being removed from the list of certified trade unions. Half of these were mining unions comprising five branches of the NUM (National Union of Mineworkers), two of NACODS (National Association of Colliery Overmen, Deputies and Shotfirers) and SCEBTA (Scottish Colliery Enginemen, Boilermen and Tradesmen's Association). Whereas the dissolution of mining unions can be attributed to the decline of that industry, most of the

Table 7.5: Last recorded membership of dissolved unions outside of mining

Union	Last recorded membership	Year of last return
Amateur and Semi-pro Sportsman's Union (ASSU)	30	2016
Association of Somerset Inseminators (ASI)	3	2017
Bus Workers Alliance (BWA)	30	2015
Federation of Professional Railway Staff (FPRS)	10	2015
Pop-Up Union	Unavailable	No return submitted
Shield Guarding Staff Association (SGSA)	779	2013
Union of Country Sports Workers (UCSW)	3,084	2015
Whatman International Staff Association (WISA)	0	2015

Source: Certification Returns, 2013–2016.

other unions dissolved over this period were small, having a membership of 30 or fewer, with several requiring further explanation (see Table 7.5).

The Shield Guarding Staff Association (SGSA) was dissolved on 9 October 2015, a decision which seemed to pre-empt the company going into administration in February 2016 (*The Gazette*, 2016). The Union of Country Sports Workers (UCSW) was dissolved following a decision taken at the organization's annual general meeting in 2015, apparently because it was no longer viable (Portwin, 2015). WISA reported 63 members in 2014, but seems to have lost all its membership by 2015 (Certification Returns, 2014, 2015), although the company still appears to be trading. Finally, the Pop-Up Union was formed at the University of Sussex by employees who were threatened with outsourcing and were unhappy at the response of the established unions. The union was set up quickly, as the name implies, and received certification in 2013; however it failed to submit any annual returns and was removed from the list of certified unions by the Certification Officer in 2015. Unfortunately all attempts to contact the union for further information during the course of the research were unsuccessful but the case illustrates the problem of forming a new union with an initial base of support that subsequently proves to be ephemeral.

The demise of the ROA further highlights some of the difficulties experienced by smaller niche unions. It was formed in 1966 and represented retired ex-military employees working in the MOD (Ministry of Defence), becoming a certified trade union in 1972 (ROA, 2013). The ROA interviewee explained that the civil service closed recruitment to the retired officer grade in 2003, with the result that the union's membership went into decline. It then relaxed its membership territories to include any MOD employee at civil service Grade D or above, who had served in the armed forces. Despite this the union then entered a terminal decline, reporting a 67.5 per cent loss of membership over the last four years of its existence (Certification Returns, 2009, 2013). In this period there were discussions of possible merger with unions including FDA, Prospect and PCS. Having failed to find a suitable merger partner the union decided to allow its membership and finances to run down to a point where it was no longer viable and was finally dissolved in 2013.

These cases serve to illustrate the difficulty in maintaining small unions which typically have no professional staff, limited resources and a declining membership. It might be questioned why these unions did not successfully conclude a transfer of engagements to a larger union. However, if the union has few members and limited assets it may not be viewed as an attractive proposition by major merging unions. Alternatively, it may be that a decision was made to wind up these unions, possibly without any consideration of merger.

Concluding discussion

In exploring the developing story of union identities this chapter highlights four important drivers to change. The merger wave of recent decades saw many niche unions absorbed into generals, which can be seen as a 'direction of travel'. Whereas amalgamations generally result in new identities and rebranding, minor merging unions tend to lose identity in the merger process, albeit for any element of sectional identity. Concurrently, a number of unions have been dissolved without successfully concluding transfers of engagements, with all but one projecting a niche union identity. Several unions have rebranded, with some following the example of Unison in adopting aspirational titles while others have non-specific titles. An implication of this is that union identity may now be less clear to potential members. However, the trend may now have abated as none of the unions changing their names in recent years, or any of the new unions listed or certified over the same period, have adopted such titles, in many cases choosing names indicating their membership territories. The development of 'new-generation' unions such as IWUGB, more clearly focused on organizing the unorganized, offers an alternative approach. These unions remain relatively small at present and while employing a distinct range of tactics, they are not considered to project a new form of niche union identity.

Although by number the vast majority of unions certified in Great Britain project a niche identity, analysis of the drivers to change raises questions as to whether British unions are becoming more 'open' (Turner, 1962) and less niche. Given that over recent years 9 of 11 unions transferring engagements did so to general unions, that all 16 dissolved unions projected a niche identity and that 4 of the 14 new unions formed over the same period adopted a general union identity, the evidence seems to confirm a trend away from niche to general union identity. However, despite this apparent direction of travel, many niche unions survive, often showing resistance to merger, while new ones continue to be formed, raising critical questions about the primacy of general unions and the persistence of niche identity (see further discussions in Chapter Nine).

As regards the major general unions, a potential criticism is that any membership growth they achieve is often attributable to transfers of engagements, raising a question as to how well they are positioned to organize the unorganized. It can be argued that the past successes of niche unions in organizing industrial, occupational and organizational niches within the labour market have provided the general unions with a ready supply of merger partners. Following this line of argument, a case can be made for general unions to support and ferment the formation of new niche unions that project occupational, industrial or organizational identities. The rationale for this is that niche unions might be more effective at breaking into new or under-organized areas of the labour market and organizing the unorganized (see further discussion in Chapter Nine).

EIGHT

Comparative Analysis of Union Identities

Introducing a comparative analysis of union identities

While the work to this point has focused upon understanding the projected identities of unions certified in Great Britain, albeit including some binational and multinational unions, this chapter explores how the multidimensional framework might be applied to unions based in five other countries and to considering what additional sources of union identity might be required. In offering this extremely limited comparative analysis it is acknowledged that it can only scratch the surface of the global experience and therefore should be regarded as a starting point for future work. Although the research reported earlier explored the projected identities of all unions certified in Great Britain, it was not possible within the limitations of this work to do such extensive research on each of the countries considered. The comparative analysis offered in this chapter therefore draws largely upon secondary source material, although it was sometimes possible to explore the websites of national union centres and of some significant unions.

The five countries examined in this chapter are China, France, Germany, Japan and the United States of America (US). In each case they were selected because they provided evidence that either utilized the sources of identity projected by unions certified in Great Britain and/or suggested additional sources which might need to be incorporated in the multidimensional framework to enable a more comprehensive comparative analysis. In exploring the manifestation of union identities and niche unionism in other countries it is recognized that different union structures exist. While the TUC provides the main trade union centre in Great Britain, albeit with regional TUCs in Scotland and Wales, many countries have multiple union centres, often reflecting the identities of their affiliates. It was therefore considered necessary to briefly explain the significance of these in relation to understanding the projected identities of their affiliates.

Union identities in China

In China a single trade union, the All-China Federation of Trade Unions (ACFTU) operates in parallel with the Chinese Communist Party (CCP), having the legal duty to 'safeguard the legal rights and interests of the employees' while 'upholding the rights and interests of the whole nation' (Cooke, 2012, p 136). However, Liu (2013) suggests that because competing trade unions are illegal, the ACFTU cannot be considered as genuinely representative of organized labour. It can be argued that representation is not the union's most important function but, rather, it is helping the party maintain social cohesion (Cooke, 2012). As a consequence of the CCP's policies of economic reform and globalization, both the ACFTU in particular, and industrial relations system in general, are under some pressure, as manifested in an increased incidence of strikes and by limited reforms (Qingjun, 2010; Zhu et al, 2011; Wen and Lin, 2014). By organizing all workers, the AFCTU can be considered as the ultimate 'true general' union, albeit that its membership territories are constrained by national boundaries. However, it must be questioned how long the Chinese state can retain this single union model within the context of a fast-changing society.

Union identities in France

In France, the trade union movement is largely divided by between five rival centres and along political and religious lines. Milner (2015, p 70) argues that 'French unions are ideologically divided and characterised by a combination of broad social justice concerns and antagonistic class relations with employers and the state'. In order to understand the identities projected by French trade unions it is necessary to gain some appreciation of the five trade union centres. The largest is the CGT (*Confédération Générale du Travail* [General Confederation of Labour]) which was founded in 1895 with revolutionary anti-capitalist policies, although these were apparently moderated in the 1990s (Laroche, 2016). The CFTC (*Confédération Française des Travailleurs Chrétiens* [French Confederation of Christian Workers]) was 'established in 1919, as a Catholic alternative to the Marxist leaning *Confédération Générale du Travail* (CGT)' (Parsons, 2013, p 190). The CGT–FO (*Confédération Générale du Travail – Force Ouvrière* [General Confederation of Labour – Workers' Force]) was formed in 1948 'following a split within the CGT in reaction to the increasing influence of the French Communist Party' (Parsons, 2013, p 190). CFDT (*Confédération Française Démocratique du Travail* [French Democratic Confederation of Labour]) 'began as a mainstream faction of the CFTC, which decided to abandon any reference to Christian social morality during its 1964 convention. While preserving a few ideas from the old CFTC ... the CFDT's statutes legitimised the role of Marxism in union action' (Laroche, 2016, p 159). Finally, the CFE–CGC (*Confédération Française de l'Encadrement – Confédération Générale des Cadres* [French Confederation of Management – General Confederation of Executives]), was formed in 1944 by unions representing management and sales representatives and developed membership benefits including a pension plan (Laroche, 2016).

In trying to understand the projected identities of French unions, the first four confederations (CGT, CFTC, CGT–FO, CFDT), might be considered as representing unions projecting a variety of 'occupational/industrial' identities, but to fully understand them it is necessary to introduce political and religious sources of union identity. In contrast, the CFE–CGC represents 'horizontal/occupational/industrial' unions. Although a federation, it perhaps has more in common with Prospect in seeking to organize managers and professionals across economic sectors. While it is beyond the scope of this work to explore the multiplicity of individual French trade union identities, taking the example of SUD–Rail (*Solidaire Unitaire et Démocratique–Rail* [Solidarity, Unity and Democracy–Rail]), at first sight it projects an industrial identity (SUD–Rail, 2019). However, deeper investigation reveals that it was formed in 1996 as a breakaway union with a distinct political agenda (Connolly, 2012). Therefore, to understand this union's niche identity it is necessary to add a political source. It could be argued that there is a 'protest union' component to the identity of this and many other French unions. However, where this term is applied to unions certified in Great Britain such as the FOA and Voice, it is because they offer a benign alternative to mainstream trade unions. In contrast, in the extremely fragmented context of French union organization it is argued here that the term is of little value, because joining almost any French trade union might be viewed as an act of protest against all others one might legitimately join.

Union identities in Germany

In Germany, industrial sector unions were established as part of post-World War II reconstruction and are affiliated to the main trade union centre organization, the DGB (*Deutscher Gewerkschaftsbund* [German Trade Union Confederation]) (Eton, 2000). While the majority of union members belong to DGB unions, a minority are organized by unions affiliated to a confederation of Christian unions, the CGB (*Christlicher Gewerkschaftsbund Deutschlands* [Christian Trade Union Confederation of Germany]), the civil service association, DBB (*Deutscher Beamtenbund* [German Civil Service Federation]), and in recent years some small professional associations (Keller and Kirsch, 2016). Therefore, in order to understand German union identities, while the DGB affiliates project industrial identities, for those of the CGB it is necessary to include a religious component, as observed in certain French unions. In contrast, the civil service union (DBB) projects a narrower industrial identity while the professional associations project 'occupational/professional' identities similar to professional unions certified in Great Britain. It might be argued that all those unions outside of the DGB project a protest union identity, given that they give their members the option of joining unions outside the mainstream of German union organization.

Union identities in Japan

In Japan the main trade union centre, Rengo, was formed in 1989 from the dissolution of two earlier federations and reports having 49 affiliates or associates (Rengo, 2019). Whereas the federations tend to comprise unions within industrial sectors, associated unions tend to represent workers in the public sector and public services. In contrast union organization in the corporate sector is dominated by enterprise-level unions. Whittaker (2013, p 248) states:

> Enterprise unions are not company unions [and that] ... enterprise union does not necessarily mean that the enterprise has only one union. Originally, many factories had separate unions, which over time were amalgamated into an enterprise union [but that] ... sometimes there were splits often around ideology and willingness to cooperate with the management.

What becomes clear in the case of Japan is that union organization is multilayered, with Rengo representing a broad range of federations and unions. While the federations bring together enterprise unions projecting organizational identities, individual unions may also project either industrial or occupational/industrial identities. As with unions in Great Britain, Japanese trade unions project a relatively complex range of identities, although rather more dominated by organizational unions and lacking the dominance of general unions.

Union identities in the United States of America

Finally, turning to the US, trade union development is to some extent resonant of that in the United Kingdom, with pre-industrial origins in craft lasting well into the twentieth century (Katz and Colvin, 2016). With the later development of industrial unions, conflict between the two traditions came to a head at the 1934 convention of the AFL (American Federation of Labor), leading the industrial unions to form a breakaway union centre, the CIO (Committee for Industrial Organization) (Tawney, 1942; Pelling, 1960). This fracture in labour organization was only resolved by the merger of AFL and CIO in 1955 to form AFL–CIO, since when it 'has been the sole umbrella union in the United States and Canada' (Farnham, 2015, p 253). It may be is seen as atypical in being both a binational trade union centre and in having many binational affiliates. The AFL–CIO currently reports having 54 affiliates (AFL–CIO, 2019). From observation of these unions' names, all appear to project an occupational and/or industrial identity. There was no evidence of any union projecting an organizational identity, although this is not to say that they do not exist in the US, but rather that none is affiliated to the AFL–CIO. Similarly, no union appeared to have membership territories beyond the US and Canada, although the Writers Guild of America East projects a subnational identity. It defines its membership territories by stating, 'Writers living east of the Mississippi River join the Writers Guild of America, East Inc. and writers living west of the Mississippi join the Writers Guild of America, West' (The Black List, 2019). However, unlike its sister union, the Writers Guild of America, West is not affiliated to AFL–CIO.

Beyond the AFL–CIO, the Teamsters are a general union, albeit with a strong membership base in transport. Founded in 1903 from two earlier unions, they describe themselves as, 'North America's strongest union' (Teamsters, 2019). The union disaffiliated from AFL–CIO in 2005 to form the backbone of a new trade union centre, CTW (Change to Win). That organization currently reports having three other affiliates, all appearing to project industrial identities (Change to Win, 2019). Also outside of AFL–CIO, the IWW, which was founded in the United States in 1905 (Pelling, 1960) with a multinational union identity, remains active in North America (IWW, 2019) (see also discussion of IWW in Chapters Three and Six). Both the Teamsters and IWW project 'protest union' identities in that they position themselves outside the main-stream of unions affiliated to the AFL–CIO. However, whereas British protest unions such as FOA and Voice offer moderate alternatives to their mainstream competitors, the Teamsters and IWW adopt more radical positions than the AFL–CIO.

Concluding discussion

Overall, this limited comparative analysis demonstrates the potential transferability of the multidimensional framework of analysis which emerged from research on unions certified in Great Britain, to unions operating in other countries. However, it is also clear that additional sources are required to under-stand union identities in certain countries, as for example in France, where some unions draw upon political and religious sources of identity. It is also clear that in some countries certain union identities predominate, as is the case with a single 'true general' union in China, industrial unions in Germany and organizational unions in Japan. Protest union identity is seen as an important component of identity in countries such as Germany and the US, where unions which tend to be either more moderate or more radical exist outside of the mainstream federations. Comparative differences are also reflected in the practice of niche unionism, whereby the different membership territories adopted in different countries determine the niche identities that their unions project. With the exception of China, a variety of union identities were observed in each country, but none showed such a diverse range as that observed in Great Britain. Having made this limited exploration of the potential for comparative application of this work, the next and final chapter turns to reviewing what has been learnt from the work and to considering critical questions that emerged from it for the future of trade union identities and niche unionism.

NINE

The Future of Union Identities and Niche Unionism

Introduction

This final chapter first explores the implications of the work for the understanding of trade union identities and niche unionism in Great Britain and beyond. As stated at the outset, this work not only seeks to develop an understanding of contemporary union identities and the role of niche unionism, but also to stimulate debate. To this end the chapter then raises a number of critical questions that emerged during the course of the research. These questions have clear implications for the future of trade union organization, union renewal and revitalization and the challenge of organizing the unorganized. The questions concern the apparent primacy of general unions, the persistence of niche unions, whether general or niche unions might be better placed to organize the unorganized and whether niche identity is an inherent barrier to niche unions expanding their membership territories.

Understanding trade union identities and niche unionism

This work argues that while much of the extant industrial relations literature is devoted to understanding aspects of trade unions, there is limited consideration of union identity and still less to the concept of niche. The approach of 'categorizers' was considered to be too rigid, although some of the established categories were absorbed into the multidimensional framework of analysis (Webb and Webb, 1894, 1902, 1920; Hughes, 1967; Hyman, 1975; Clegg, 1979; Heery and Kelly, 1994; Visser, 2012). The work of those who employ more 'flexible approaches' was also considered but these were judged variously outdated, not entirely relevant or inadequate for addressing the questions of union identity and niche explored in this work (Turner, 1962; Blackburn 1967; Undy et al, 1981; Hyman, 1994, 2001; Hodder and Edwards, 2015). Blackburn's (1967) seven elements of unionateness were considered at some length because of the inevitable overlap with this work, but were found to be more or less relevant to understanding contemporary union identities. Turner's (1962) open-to-closed continuum was the most directly relevant to this work, but it was considered that a single dimension was inadequate for understanding the complexity of contemporary union identities and that a multidimensional framework of analysis was required (see discussions in Chapters One and Two).

The multidimensional framework incorporates sources of union identity derived both from existing categorizations and through analysis of data from the research conducted on unions certified in Great Britain. Analysis of the research data led to the recognition of primary, secondary and additional sources of identity from which union identities can be understood. Operationalizing the multidimensional framework recognized that beyond 'true general', all other union identities contain at least some element of niche identity. Unions which are not general in character are termed 'niche unions' and, by reference to the multidimensional framework, it is possible to identify how an individual niche union's identity is constructed. Application of the multidimensional framework makes it possible for the sources of identity to be applied flexibly, rather than as absolute concepts, avoiding the rigidity of categorization. The multidimensional framework therefore explains what 'closed' (following Turner, 1962) means in relation to the projected identities of contemporary unions. In addition to niche union identity, the work also recognizes the wider concept of 'niche unionism' which encompasses both niche unions and larger, and particularly general unions, with sectionalized structures that afford members some element of niche identity. However, what is presented is inevitably a 'snapshot of a moving picture' and it is acknowledged that the multidimensional framework may need to be developed in order to recognize unforeseen developments in union identities (see discussion in Chapter Two).

Further analysis of unions certified in Great Britain under the broad headings of general, industrial/occupational, organizational and geographical provides more detailed evidence (see Chapters Three–Six). However, with union identities changing over time, the work considered the impact of four drivers to change, namely merger, rebranding, the formation of new unions and the dissolution of existing ones (see also discussion in Chapter Seven). Finally, the limited application of the multidimensional framework to unions based in other countries demonstrates that while it is generally applicable, further sources of union identity need to be included. This limited comparative analysis suggests that there is potential for further work, conducting primary source research on union websites and including a wider range of countries (see discussion in Chapter Eight).

Overall this work has sought to develop the understanding of contemporary union identities and niche unionism through the construction and operationalizing of the multidimensional framework, detailed consideration of union identities, changes in union identities and limited comparative analysis. However, this chapter now turns to explore critical questions that emerged through the course of the work and the implications of these for the future of union organization in general and the problem of organizing the unorganized in particular.

Is the primacy of general unions inevitable?

The success of the major general unions in organizing around half of UK union membership (BEIS, 2019) and accommodating an extremely diverse range of minor merging unions within their sectionalized structures raises a question as to whether the primacy of general unions is inevitable, and, by implication, whether niche unions can survive. It is suggested in this work that there is a 'direction of travel' from niche to general unionism. However, it was also recognized that this was made possible by the past successes of minor merging unions in organizing niches within the labour market. It might be argued the major generals could eventually absorb most remaining niche unions into their ranks. This trend might be seen as one of the homogenization of union identities, leading logically to an endpoint where niche union identity disappears. In contrast to this trend of general unionism, some mergers have consolidated niche union identity within industrial sectors, as exemplified by those that formed NEU, RMT and UCU.

Although major general unions have frequently shown membership growth over recent decades, much of this can be attributed to transfers of engagements and therefore even when their memberships grow it is hard to assess how well they are performing in terms of organizing the unorganized. While major general unions can provide some element of niche identity to minor merging unions through their occupational or trade sections, this is dependent on the flexibility of the major merging union (see discussion in Chapter Three). Some transfers of engagements may lead to a more significant loss of identity, as in the case of that experienced by APAP when transferring engagements to GMB. In contrast, a stronger identity can be retained where the major merging union shows greater flexibility, as demonstrated by the 'Connect' section formed within Prospect to accommodate the union of the same name. A criticism of the trend towards general unionism is that the general unions may become repositories for failing unions. This is exemplified by recent transfers of engagements that have included that of UCATT to Unite and BECTU to Prospect. Both of these mergers would seem to be the result of casualization in their respective industries and the resulting difficulties in maintaining union organization. While it is not possible to monitor the fate of minor merging unions following their transfers of engagements, it is possible that their membership might continue to decline, unless perhaps the greater resources of the general union are harnessed to improve recruitment.

The trend of merger into general unions raises a question as to why there needs to be more than one general union, and if so whether there should be a megamerger between major generals. Given that two major generals project some niche characteristics, with Prospect seeking to organize the higher echelons of employment horizontally and Unison the public sector and public services vertically, they might be considered unlikely merger partners. In contrast, Unite and GMB as 'true generals' offer a more promising fit, given their diverse range of industrial sections and mix of public and private sector workers. However, the concept of megamergers raises a question as to whether there might be an optimal size for general unions, beyond which they might become less effective. As their memberships become increasingly diverse a further question arises as to how effectively they can continue to accommodate the needs of disparate groups within their sectionalized structures. Further, there is the question of the dominance of a 'mega' union in relation to its TUC and Labour Party affiliation, previously raised by Undy (2008) in relation to the formation of Unite. Whether a megamerger is either possible or desirable are questions ultimately beyond the limitations of this work, but the concept would seem to deserve further exploration given the overall implications for the future shape of trade union organization (see also discussion in Chapter Three).

In contrast to the major generals, the development of new minor general unions includes the formation of Community by merger and the development of 'new-generation' unions. Community, which was formed by merger of industrial/occupational unions and has become a successful major merging union by achieving transfers of engagements from unions including the SUWBBS and UFS (see discussion in Chapter Three). Several new unions have also adopted a general union identity, including two 'new-generation' unions (IWUGB and UVW), but it remains to be seen whether these will be viable in the long term and continue to make a significant contribution to organizing the unorganized. It became clear during the research that new niche unions continued to be formed and that many existing ones were resistant to the merger with a major general union, seeing it as a last resort should the organization get into financial problems. In contrast to the general unions, niche unions tend to tailor what they offer to their members' needs and may also supply their identity needs. Therefore, despite the dominant position of major general unions and the formation of new minor generals, there are multiple reasons to expect the persistence of niche unions, to which this discussion now turns.

How can we explain the persistence of niche unions?

The research reported earlier in this work established that only 16 per cent of unions projected a general identity (see Chapter Two), and therefore the vast majority of unions certified in Great Britain project a niche identity. Although the statistics reported earlier show an increase in general union identity as a percentage of the whole (see Chapter Two), this is largely because of the formation of new general unions such as the EFWU, ESOSTU and UVW. Despite the loss of niche unions through transfers of engagements and dissolutions, new niche unions continue to emerge to replace them, such as AUE, ALCC (Association of Local Council Clerks) and CAIWU.

A number of possible explanations for the persistence of niche unions that emerged from the research are discussed in this section, although it is recognized that these are not necessarily either exhaustive or mutually exclusive.

Niche unions by their nature organize niches within the labour market in membership territories defined by one or more of the primary sources of union identity. Their members may have specific needs which can be better served by a niche union, as demonstrated by professional unions such as ACB/ FCS, AEP and BADN and occupational unions including PFA, NARS and WGGB. Their survival suggests that a perceived need for union organization remains within a defined niche, albeit that it may be broadened over time to organize other groups, as is the case with Accord and Advance, or through merger, as exemplified by ACB/FCS and WGGB. While niche unions often provide merger partners for major merging unions (Waddington, 1995; Undy 2008), their persistence deters general unions from organizing within certain niches of the labour market, supporting Turner's (1962) assertion that general unions are constrained from being truly general by the existence of other unions. A niche union may also benefit from a historic legacy where it is established and better placed to organize that particular niche, as for example within an occupational (PFA, NARS, WGGB), organizational (Advance), professional (AEP, BADN), sub-occupational (NSEAD) or subnational (EIS, SSTA, UCAC) niche.

While the merger process of recent decades suggests a 'direction of travel' from the formation of niche unions to their eventual absorption into general unions, many interviewees reported their union as being resistant to merger, frequently seeing independence as an organizational objective. However, merger with a general union was sometimes acknowledged as being a last resort should the union not have sufficient financial resources to survive as an independent entity, confirming earlier work (Willman et al, 1993; Waddington, 1995; Undy, 2008). That numerous niche unions have transferred engagements to general unions over recent decades cannot be disputed, but for many of these it seems to have been a defensive measure. Therefore it is argued here that where niche unions make independence an organizational objective, have a secure membership base and remain financially solvent, they may be able to avoid the trend of merger with a general union.

While the fortunes of organizational unions are frequently dependent upon those of the employing organization or organizations, they have tended to be adept at negotiating transfers of engagements to larger industry or general unions, and bringing their members into the mainstream of trade unionism. This also suggests a 'direction of travel' from their formation, through achieving independence and certification as trade unions, to absorption within the mainstream of trade unionism. Therefore it is argued here that they should not be ignored as a potential source of union renewal and regeneration and that the formation of new organizational unions might be encouraged by established unions, which might ultimately be the beneficiaries of transfers of engagements.

Niche unions may also satisfy their members' needs for a derived identity and particularly so where they organize a single occupation (PFA and WGGB) or profession (AEP and BADN). This might be an issue for certain niche unions in relation to their members' need to maintain their status position. Lockwood (1958, p 208) saw status as, 'the more subtle distinctions which stem from the values that men set on each other's activities', while members of higher status occupations may also be seen as forming a 'labour aristocracy' (Hobsbawm, 1964). Examples include the position of the train drivers' union ASLEF and the broadly based transport industry union RMT, the pilots' union BALPA and Unite, which organizes many cabin crew, and similarly the position of the BMA in relation to Unison, which represents many health service employees. In each case, where the higher status union organizes horizontally, and the industrial or general union organizes vertically, the latter is effectively blocked by the higher status union.

The need to maintain members' status position might also be expected to form a barrier to merger between higher and lower status unions.

Theoretical explanations (explored in Chapter One) can be applied to understanding the identity needs of union members. These include social identity theory, which suggests that social identity is primarily drawn from group membership (Ashforth and Mael, 1989; Brown, 2000) and that through membership individuals may derive a positive self-identity (Turner and Tajfel, 1986); self-categorization theory, which explores the extent to which individuals define their own social group or relationship to other groups (Hogg et al, 1990); and identity theory, which relates to the roles and behaviour of individuals in society (Hogg et al, 1995). Drawing upon these theories it is suggested here that social identity and societal roles can be derived or confirmed by union membership when unions project a distinct occupational or professional identity, such as that of ASLEF, BALPA or BMA. This derived social identity may lead to the individual being seen as part of an 'in-group' as opposed to an 'out-group' (Brown, 2000; Budd, 2011), although this might also be considered as having a broader application to trade unions, as when non-members are viewed as 'free riders' or strike breakers as 'blacklegs'.

This then raises a question as to whether any occupational or professional union might be viewed as effectively maintaining a closed shop, despite its gradual abolition under law in the 1980s (Tuckman, 2018). The research interviews revealed that certain unions claimed extremely high membership densities. The PFA suggested that 100 per cent of players were members, while AEP claimed to have the majority of practitioners in membership. What became clear was that where niche unions achieve a significant membership together with a certain status, joining may become a social norm. However, it could be argued conversely that where these unions offer comprehensive benefits tailored to the needs of their members, there is a strong instrumental motivation for membership which should also be considered (see later discussion in this section).

Beyond occupational identity, unions projecting both organizational and subnational identities can also be seen as providing their members with some element of social identity. Where organizational unions such as PPSA or NGSU include the name of the employer in their title members might see themselves as belonging to something internal to the company rather than an external trade union, even though the union holds a certificate of independence. However, where organizational unions such as Advance and Accord adopt aspirational titles, the extent to which members derive a social identity from these unions' association with the employer may be more variable. Whereas Advance employs the strapline, 'The only union dedicated to the people in Santander bank UK', no strapline was observed by Accord, which has a more diffused multi-organizational identity. The subnational unions were all observed to include a geographical component in their projected identity. In the case of three Scottish and Welsh education unions (AHDS, SSTA and UCAC), it was clear that a subnational identity formed a strong part of their niche identity. Therefore it could be considered that members might derive some sense of social identity by joining these unions rather than those 'national' education unions with geographically non-specific identities.

In contrast to social identity and self-categorization theories which relate to psychological predisposition, identity theory explores the roles and behaviour of individuals in society (Hogg et al, 1995). Returning to earlier examples, it might be that having the role of a train driver, doctor or airline pilot might not only provide the individual with a distinct role in society, but also provides a set of anticipated norms of behaviour. It might be that members prefer a union that understands the role they occupy in order to obtain specialized advice and support. For example, while it could be argued that any competent trade union official should be able to represent any union member in a disciplinary case, a train driver, doctor or airline pilot might perhaps hope for representation from an organization reflecting their role identity and with a more specialized knowledge of their occupation.

The provision of specialized benefit packages, tailored to the needs of niche memberships that would not be available from a general union, provides instrumental reasons for niche membership. This was observed to be particularly so in the case of niche unions that serve a distinct occupation (NUJ, PFA and WGGB) or profession (ACB/FCS, AEP and BADN). Many niche unions provide services including access to specialized information on technical subjects, professional journals, telephone helplines and support for CPD. Occupational and profession unions also tend to have concerns over occupational and professional regulation and are frequently involved in lobbying government and statutory bodies on behalf of their members. Access to specialized benefits together with individual and collective representation over occupational and professional issues can therefore be cited as important factors in explaining the persistence of many niche unions.

While it is acknowledged that these reasons may not be exhaustive in explaining the persistence of niche unions, it is argued that they provide significant cause to believe that many niche unions can be expected to survive for the foreseeable future, unless or until they perceive an advantage in merging, or merge of necessity. Although major general unions may offer greater resources and scale economies, they cannot accommodate all the disparate needs of niche union members and especially so where niche unions tailor what they offer to the particular requirements of an occupation or profession. The survival of niche unions against the trend of merger and general unionism over recent decades holds a number of implications for union organization in general and for general unions in particular and provokes the next question as to whether general or niche unions are better placed to organize the unorganized.

Are general or niche unions better placed to organize the unorganized?

It was never the purpose of this work to argue that either niche or general unions might be more effective in organizing the unorganized. On one hand it could be argued that major general unions are better placed to do this because they are likely to have greater resources than most niche unions. Alternatively it might be considered that niche unions, having more specialized knowledge of their defined niches, are better placed to recruit, service and retain members. Union organization can be seen as falling into two areas, with the first being to improve organization within existing membership territories and the second to expand into unorganized areas of the labour market. While it might be argued that the first area should be a priority for all unions in order to maintain their established position, the second raises the question of whether general or niche unions might be in a better position to organize in unorganized areas.

In organizing around a niche identity, niche unions may have certain advantages in bringing knowledge or expertise of a particular industrial, occupational, professional, organizational or geographical niche within the labour market. Organizational unions may benefit from some identification with the employer while subnational unions may gain some advantage from their geographical identities, as demonstrated by Scottish and Welsh education unions. As reported earlier, niche unions may offer tailored benefits and may supply certain identity needs, to a far greater extent than might be derived from sectional membership of a major general union. However, the success of niche unions in attracting and retaining members was found to be highly variable. Whereas some niche unions had relatively stable membership over recent years (Advance, AEP, PFA), some showed substantial increases (ASCL, BADN FOA, NARS, Nautilus, WGGB) while others struggled to recruit or are in decline (NUJ, SSTA, Voice). Therefore, despite the relative success of certain niche unions, it cannot be argued that niche union identity necessarily provides an antidote to decline or a prescription for union renewal but rather that it has proved successful for certain unions that either have secure membership territories including AEP, BADN, NARS, PFA and WGGB, or are able to compete with other unions organizing in their niche such as ASCL, FOA and Nautilus.

More recently, the formation of what are termed in this work 'new-generation' unions, such as CAIWU, IWUGB and UVW, raises a question as to the voracity of both established niche and general unions in organizing unorganized sectors of the labour market. While some new-generation unions have achieved notable successes by employing a particular range of tactics, they are relatively small and it remains to be seen whether they or established unions prove the more successful in organizing the unorganized over the coming years. The success of new-generation unions in focusing their activity directly on precarious workers also provokes the question which is addressed next: whether established niche unions are inextricably locked into their established membership territories to the point that this forms a barrier to expanding them.

Is niche identity a barrier to expanding membership territories?

A potential problem with niche union identity is that the more narrowly the union defines its membership territories, the harder it may be to expand these into new areas. This was clearly demonstrated by professional unions such as AEP and BADN and occupational unions including ASLEF and PFA. As these unions frequently tailor benefits to the needs of their members and may satisfy certain identity needs, any expansion of their membership territories might dilute their niche identity. However, this may be less of a problem for unions projecting an industrial identity, where the barrier to expansion is more likely to be the existence of other unions. This is exemplified in the rail industry, where territorial expansion by RMT is constrained by the existence of unions including ASLEF and TSSA.

Some niche unions have demonstrated the ability to broaden their membership territories in order to recruit more widely within an industry, as demonstrated by NARS within the racing industry and FRSA within fire and rescue. Similarly, several organizational unions, including Accord, Affinity and Aegis, have widened their membership territories to organize in other institutions within the banking and finance sector. In each case these organizational unions seem to be in transition from projecting organizational to industrial identities, perhaps seeking to avoid absorption into the 'Finance and Law' section of Unite. Action by McDonald's workers organized by the BFAWU demonstrated the willingness of an established union to break into a previously unorganized area. Some niche unions, such as ACB/FCS and WGGB, have expanded their membership territories by merger. Whereas subnational and binational geographical unions showed no intention of expanding their membership territories, the formation of Nautilus as a multinational union raises the possibility of further cross-border mergers.

The major general unions are normally able to offer minor merging unions some element of niche identity through their existing sections and may even create new ones to facilitate a transfer of engagements. However, the question for major general unions might be whether the identities of their existing sections create a barrier to organizing in new areas, and if so whether they need to create new sections or redefine existing ones to organize the unorganized more effectively. The rebranding of Community to become a true general union and organize outside its traditional membership territories (Community, 2015) and the development of Unite's 'Community' section to recruit beyond formal employment (Unite, 2013) might in different ways be considered as attempts to break out of established membership territories.

Overall the evidence on the question of whether niche identity is a barrier to expanding membership territories is mixed. Where unions seek to organize more widely it may be a defensive reaction to their established niche coming under pressure, as demonstrated by the experience of organizational unions in the banking and finance industry. In contrast, there are more positive signs of attempts to recruit more widely, as for example the campaign of the BFAWU and the formation of Unite's 'Community' section. However, this works suggests that an opportunity exists for more unions to consider how and where they might expand their membership territories in order to recruit in unorganized areas of the labour market and to contribute to the organization of the unorganized.

Concluding discussion

In drawing together the analysis offered both in this chapter and in the work overall, it is argued that the development of the multidimensional framework offers new insights into contemporary identities of unions certified in Great Britain. In doing so it goes beyond earlier categorizations or flexible frameworks, most of which do not directly address questions of union identity or niche. It is anticipated that the multidimensional framework may be developed over time to accommodate future developments in the identities of unions certified in Great Britain and for comparative analysis of the identities of unions based in other countries. Operationalizing the multidimensional framework makes possible the recognition of niche union identity and therefore of niche unions. This recognition in turn exposes a clear distinction between niche and general unions, and a further distinction between true generals which are prepared to accept almost any member and niche generals which project some niche characteristics by restricting membership horizontally or vertically. The term 'niche unionism' is introduced to encompass both niche unions and the niche identity derived from the industrial/occupational sections of some larger unions, and particularly major general unions.

This work raises certain critical questions explored in this chapter. It can be argued that major general unions provide greater resources, a repository for declining unions and are able to accommodate virtually any type of worker. Conversely, niche unions offer members specialized advice, support and benefits tailored closely to their needs and may also contribute to their identity needs. Some niche unions, and particularly those representing distinct occupations and professions, seem relatively constrained by their niche identity, whereas industry unions are more constrained by the existence of other unions. However, many niche unions have secured a base of membership within the labour market and new niche unions continue to be formed. Paradoxically it is the past successes of niche unions, projecting occupational, industrial and organizational identities, organizing niches within the labour market and then transferring engagements, which has contributed so much to the strength of the major general unions. Therefore, it is argued that despite an apparent direction of travel towards general unionism, part of the answer to the problem of organizing the unorganized might be to ferment the formation of new niche unions. Similarly, the development of 'new-generation' unions, while not projecting a new form of union identity, may be seen as an important development in employing a distinct range of tactics focused directly on precarious workers.

Finally, while this book attempts to bring new insight and understanding to the questions of union identity and niche unionism, it is not presented as a last word, but rather it is hoped it will be a starting point for discussion and debate, both within the academic field of industrial relations and the trade union movement itself, contributing something of value to the much wider debates and discussions on union organization and the problem of organizing the unorganized.

References

Ackers, P. (1995). 'Change in trade unions since 1945: A response to Heery and Kelly', *Work, Employment & Society*, 9(1): 147–154.

Ackers, P. (2015) 'Trade unions as professional associations', in Johnstone, S. and Ackers, P. (eds), *Finding a Voice at Work? New Perspectives on Employment Relations*, Oxford: Oxford University Press, pp 95–126.

Ackroyd, S. (2011) 'Research designs for realist research', in Buchanan, D.A. and Bryman, A. (eds), *The SAGE Handbook of Organisational Research Methods*, London: Sage, pp 532–548.

Advance (2019) *Who Are Advance*, www.advance-union.org

AFL–CIO (2019) *Our Affiliated Unions*, www.changetowin.org/about-us/#affiliates

Albert, S. and Whetten, D.A. (1985) 'Organizational identity', *Research in Organizational Behavior*, 7: 263–295.

Allen, V.L. (1958) 'The National Union of Police and Prison Officers', *The Economic History Review*, 11(1): 133–143.

Allen, V.L. (1963) 'Valuations and historical interpretation: a case study', *British Journal of Sociology*, 14(1): 48–58.

Alvesson, M. and Karreman, D. (2011) *Qualitative Research and Theory Development: Mystery as Method*, London: Sage.

Ashforth, B. and Mael, F. (1989) 'Social identity theory and the organization', *Academy of Management Review*, 14(1): 20–39.

Balmer, J.M. (1998) 'Corporate identity and the advent of corporate marketing', *Journal of Marketing Management*, 14(8): 963–996.

Balmer, J.M. (2008) 'Identity based views of the corporation: insights from corporate identity, organisational identity, social identity, visual identity, corporate brand identity and corporate image', *European Journal of Marketing*, 42(9/10): 879–906.

Balmer, J.M. and Soenen, G.B. (1999) 'The acid test of corporate identity management™', *Journal of Marketing Management*, 15(1–3): 69–92.

Bean, R. (1980) 'Police unrest, unionization and the 1919 strike in Liverpool', *Journal of Contemporary History*, 15(4): 633–653.

BEIS (2019) *Trade Union Membership 2018: Statistical Bulletin*, Department for Business, Energy and Industrial Strategy, www.gov.uk/government/statistics/trade-union-statistics-2018

Blackburn, R.M. (1967) *Union Character and Social Class: A Study of White-Collar Trade Unionism*, London: Batsford.

Blanchflower, D.G. and Bryson, A. (2009) 'Trade union decline and the economics of the workplace', in Brown, W., Bryson, A., Forth, J. and Whitfield, K. (eds), *The Evolution of the Modern Workplace*, Cambridge: Cambridge University Press, pp 48–73.

Boxall, P. and Purcell, J. (2008) *Strategy and Human Resource Management,* (2nd edn) Basingstoke: Palgrave Macmillan.

Brown, R. (2000) 'Social identity theory: Past achievements, current problems and future challenges', *European Journal of Social Psychology*, 30(6): 745–778.

Brown, W., Bryson, A. and Forth, J. (2009) 'Competition and the retreat from collective bargaining', in Brown, W., Bryson, A., Forth, J. and Whitfield, K. (eds) *The Evolution of the Modern Workplace*, Cambridge: Cambridge University Press, pp 22–47.

Bryman, A. and Bell, E. (2011) *Social Research Methods* (3rd edn), Oxford: Oxford University Press.

Budd, J.W. (2011) *The Thought of Work*, Ithaca, NY: Cornell University Press.

Burghausen, M. and Balmer, J. (2015) 'Corporate heritage identity stewardship: A corporate marketing perspective', *European Journal of Marketing*, 49(1/2): 22–61.

Certification Officer (2008) *Annual Report of the Certification Officer 2007–2008*, www.certoffice.org/annualReport/index.cfm?pageID=annual

Certification Officer (2009) *Annual Report of the Certification Officer 2008–2009*, www.certoffice.org/annualReport/index.cfm?pageID=annual

Certification Officer (2010) *Annual Report of the Certification Officer 2009–2010*, www.gov.uk/government/publications/annual-report-of-the-certification-officer-2009–2010

Certification Officer (2011) *Annual Report of the Certification Officer 2010–2011*, www.gov.uk/government/publications/annual-report-of-the-certification-officer-2010–2011

Certification Officer (2012) *Annual Report of the Certification Officer 2011–2012*, www.gov.uk/government/publications/annual-report-of-the-certification-officer-2011–2012

Certification Officer (2013) *Annual Report of the Certification Officer 2012–2013*, www.gov.uk/government/publications/annual-report-of-the-certification-officer-2012–2013

Certification Officer (2014) *Annual Report of the Certification Officer 2013–2014*, www.gov.uk/government/publications/annual-report-of-the-certification-officer-2013–2014

Certification Officer (2015) *Annual Report of the Certification Officer 2014–2015*, www.gov.uk/government/publications/annual-report-of-the-certification-officer-2014–2015

Certification Officer (2016) *Annual Report of the Certification Officer 2015–2016*, www.gov.uk/government/publications/annual-report-of-the-certification-officer-2015–2016

Certification Officer (2018) *Annual Report of the Certification Officer 2017–2018*, www.gov.uk/government/publications/annual-report-of-the-certification-officer-2017–2018

Certification Officer (2019a) *Annual Report of the Certification Officer 2018–2019*, www.gov.uk/government/publications/annual-report-of-the-certification-officer-2018–2019

Certification Officer (2019b) *Recent Amendments to the Official List of Trade Unions and Official List of Employers' Associations*, www.gov.uk/government/news/certification-officer-amendments-to-the-lists.

Certification Officer for Northern Ireland (2019) *Annual Report of the Certification Officer for Northern Ireland 2017–2018*, www.nicertoffice.org.uk/documents/annual-report-2017-2018

Certification Returns (2009–18) *Official List and Schedule of Trade Unions and Their Annual Returns*, Certification Officer, www.gov.uk/government/publications/public-list-of-active-trade-unions-official-list-and-schedule

Change to Win (2019) *About Us*, www.changetowin.org/about-us

Clegg, H.A. (1979) *The Changing System of Industrial Relations in Great Britain*, Oxford: Blackwell.

Clegg, H.A., Fox, A. and Thompson, A.F. (1985) *A History of British Trade Unions Since 1889: 1911–1933*, Oxford: Clarendon Press.

Community (2015) *Who We Help*, https://community-tu.org/who-we-help

Connolly, H. and Darlington, R. (2012) 'Radical political unionism in France and Britain: A comparative study of SUD-Rail and the RMT', *European Journal of Industrial Relations*, 18(3): 235–250.

Cooke, F.L. (2012) *Human Resource Management in China: New Trends and Practices*, Abingdon: Routledge.

Dalgic, T. and Leeuw, M. (1994) 'Niche marketing revisited: Concept, applications and some European cases', *European Journal of Marketing*, 28(4): 39–55.

Darlington, R. (2012) 'The interplay of structure and agency dynamics in strike activity', *Employee Relations*, 34(5): 518–533.

Darlington, R. and Dobson, J. (2013) 'Objective but not detached: Partisanship in industrial relations research', *Capital and Class*, 37(2): 285–297.

Dix, G., Sisson, K. and Forth, A. (2009) 'Conflict at work: The changing pattern of disputes', in Brown, W., Bryson, A., Forth, J. and Whitfield, K. (eds), *The Evolution of the Modern Workplace*, Cambridge: Cambridge University Press, 176–200.

Elton, C. (1927) *Animal Ecology*, London: Sidgwick and Jackson.

Eton, J. (2000) *Comparative Employment Relations: An Introduction,* Cambridge: Polity Press.

Farnham, D. (2015) *The Changing Faces of Employment Relations: Global, Comparative and Theoretical Perspectives,* London: Palgrave.

Gall, G. (1997) 'Developments in trade unionism in the financial sector in Britain', *Work, Employment and Society,* 11(2): 219–235.

Gall, G. (2001) 'From adversarialism to partnership?', *Employee Relations,* 23(4): 353–375.

Gall, G. (2007) 'Playing the name game', *Morning Star,* 11 October.

Gall, G. (2017) 'The new radical independent unions – is small necessarily beautiful', [blog] 13 November, www.huffingtonpost. co.uk/gregor-gall/the-new-radical-independe_b_18529226.html

Gennard, J. (2009) 'A new emerging trend? Cross border trade union mergers', *Employee Relations,* 31(1): 5–8.

Hannan, M.T., Carroll, G.R. and Pólos, L. (2003) 'The organizational niche', *Sociological Theory,* 21(4): 309–340.

Hartsthorne, C. (1980) 'James's empirical pragmatism', *American Journal of Theology and Philosophy,* 1(1): 14–20.

He, H. and Brown, A.D. (2013) 'Organisational identity and organisational identification: A review of the literature and suggestions for future research', *Group and Organisational Management,* 38(1): 3–35.

Heery, E. and Kelly, J. (1994) 'Professional, participative and managerial unionism: An Interpretation of change in trade unions,' *Work, Employment & Society,* 8(1): 1–22.

Hobsbawm, E.J. (1964) 'Artisan or labour aristocrat?' *The Economic History Review,* 37(3): 355–372.

Hobsbawm, E.J. (1967) 'Trade union history 1', *The Economic History Review,* 20(2): 358–364.

Hodder, A. (2015) 'Young and unionised in the UK? Insights from the public sector', *Employee Relations,* 37(3): 314–332.

Hodder, A. and Edwards, P. (2015) 'The essence of trade unions: Understanding identity, ideology and purpose', *Work, Employment and Society,* 29(5): 843–854.

Hogg, M.A., Turner, J.C. and Davidson, B. (1990) 'Polarized norms and social frames of reference: A test of the self-categorization theory of group polarization', *Basic and Applied Social Psychology*, 11(1): 77–100.

Hogg, M.A., Terry, D.J. and White, K.M. (1995) 'A tale of two theories: A critical comparison of identity theory with social identity theory', *Social Psychology Quarterly*, 58(4): 255–269.

Holgate, J. (2013) 'Community organising in the UK: A 'new' approach for trade unions?', *Economic and Industrial Democracy*, 36(3): 431–455.

Hughes, J. (1967) 'Trade union structure and government', *Royal Commission on Trade Unions and Employers Associations, Research Paper 5, Part 1, Structure and Development*, London: HMSO.

Hyman, R. (1975) *Industrial Relations: A Marxist Introduction*, London: Macmillan Press.

Hyman, R. (1994) 'Theory and industrial relations', *British Journal of Industrial Relations*, 32(2): 165–180.

Hyman, R. (2001) *Understanding European Trade Unionism: Between Market, Class and Society*, London: Sage.

Irish Congress of Trade Unions (2019) *Mission & Objectives*, www.ictu.ie/about

IWUGB (2019) *About Us*, https://iwgb.org.uk/page/about/about

IWW (2019) *About the IWW*, www.iww.org/content/about-iww

Katz, H.C. and Colvin, A.J.S. (2016) 'Employment relations in the United States', in Bamber, G.J., Lansbury, R.D., Wailes, N. and Wright, C.F. (eds), *International and Comparative Employment Relations: National Regulation, Global Changes* (6th edn), London: Sage, pp 49–74.

Keller, B.K. and Kirsch, A. (2016) 'Employment relations in Germany', in Bamber, G.J., Lansbury, R.D., Wailes, N. and Wright, C.F. (eds), *International and Comparative Employment Relations: National Regulation, Global Changes* (6th edn), London: Sage, pp 179–207.

Labour Party (2019) https://labour.org.uk/people/unions

Laroche, P. (2016) 'Employment relations in France', in Bamber, G.J., Lansbury, R.D., Wailes. N. and Wright, C.F. (eds), *International and Comparative Employment Relations: National Regulation, Global Changes* (6th edn), London: Sage, pp 153–178.

Liu, M. (2013) 'China', in Frege, C. and Kelly, J. (eds), *Comparative Employment Relations in the Global Economy*, Abingdon: Routledge, pp 324–347.

Lockwood, D. (1958) *The Blackcoated Worker: A Study in Class Consciousness*, London: Unwin University Books.

Lyddon, D. (2009) 'Strikes: Industrial conflict under New Labour', in Daniels, G. and McIlroy, J. (eds), *Trade Unions in a Neoliberal World*, London: Routledge, pp 316–341.

Marchington, M. and Wilkinson, A. (2012) *Human Resource Management at Work* (5th edn), London: Chartered Institute of Personnel and Development.

McIlroy, J. and Daniels, G. (2009) 'An anatomy of British trade unionism since 1997: Organisation, structure and factionalism', in Daniels, G. and McIlroy, J. (eds) *Trade Unions in a Neoliberal World*, London: Routledge, pp 126–164.

Miller, J. (2010) *The 1975 Stable Lads Strike*, Working Lives Project, London: Trades Union Congress.

Milner, S. (2015) *Comparative Employment Relations: France, Germany and Britain*, London: Palgrave.

Moore, S. (2011) *New Trade Union Activism: Class Consciousness or Social Identity*, London: Palgrave Macmillan.

Morton, A.L. and Tate, G. (1979) *The British Labour Movement*, London: Lawrence and Wishart.

Musson, A.E. (1976) 'Craft unions, welfare benefits, and the case for trade union law reform, 1867–75: A comment', *The Economic History Review*, 29(4): 626–630.

Nautilus. (2013) *Our Union*, www.nautilusint.org/en

Parsons, N. (2013) 'France', in Frege, C. and Kelly, J. (eds), *Comparative Employment Relations in the Global Economy,* Abingdon: Routledge, pp 187–205.

Pelling, H. (1960) *American Labor*, Chicago: University of Chicago Press.

Pelling, H. (1976) *A History of British Trade Unionism* (3rd edn), Harmondsworth: Penguin.

Pollert, A. (2010) 'Spheres of collectivism: Group action and perspectives on trade unions among the low-paid unorganized with problems at work', *Capital and Class*, 34(1): 115–125.

Portwin, P. (2015) 'Country sports trade union to be dissolved', *Horse and Hound*, [online] 12 May, www.horseandhound.co.uk/news/union-of-country-sports-workers-492821#zkQyFhYrskKDijFX.99

Prospect (2019) *Who Are Prospect?*, www.prospect.org.uk/about/who

Qingjun, W. (2010) 'Establishing trade unions within foreign companies in China', *Employee Relations*, 32(4): 349–363.

Rengo (2019) *About RENGO*, www.jtuc-rengo.org/about/affiliates. html

ROA (2013) www.roa-uk.co.uk [Accessed 15 July 2013]

Robinson, J. (2019) 'PDA Union wins vote to represent Boots pharmacists', *The Pharmaceutical Journal*, [online] 12 March, www.pharmaceutical-journal.com/news-and-analysis/news/pda-union-wins-vote-to-represent-boots-pharmacists/20206274.article?firstPass=false

Robson, C, (2002) *Real World Research: A Resource for Social Scientists and Practitioner-Researchers* (2nd edn), Oxford: Blackwell Publishing.

Ross, C. (2013) 'New unions in the UK: The vanguard or the rearguard of the union movement?', *Industrial Relations Journal*, 44(1): 78–94.

Seifert, R. and Mather, K. (2013) 'Neo-liberalism at work: A case study of the reform of the emergency services in the UK', *Review of Radical Political Economics*, 45(4): 456–462.

Simms, M. and Charlwood, A. (2010) 'Trade unions: Power and influence in a changed context', in Colling, T. and Terry, M. (eds) *Industrial Relations Theory and Practice* (3rd edn), Chichester: John Wiley and Sons, pp 125–148.

Simms, M., Holgate, J. and Heery, E. (2013) *Union Voices: Tactics and Tensions in UK Organizing*, Ithaca, NY: Cornell University Press.

REFERENCES

Simms, M., Holgate, J. and Roper, C. (2019) 'The Trades Union Congress 150 years on: A review of the organising challenges and responses to the changing nature of work', *Employee Relations: The International Journal*, 41(2): 331–343.

Skyshare (2019) *Frequently Asked Questions*, http://skyshare.eu/skyshare_faq.php

Smith, P. (1995) 'Notes and issues: Debate: Change in British trade unions since 1945', *Work, Employment and Society*, 9(1): 137–146.

SUD–Rail (2019) *SUD RAIL, un syndicalisme Solidaire, Unitaire, Démocratique!* (Solidarity, unitarian, democratic unionism), https://solidaires.org/SUD-RAIL-un-syndicalisme-Solidaire-Unitaire-Democratique

Tailby, S. and Pollert, A. (2011) 'Non-unionized young workers and organizing the unorganized', *Economic and Industrial Democracy*, 32(3): 499–522.

Tapia, M. (2013) 'Marching to different tunes: Commitment and culture as mobilizing mechanisms of trade unions and community organizations', *British Journal of Industrial Relations*, 51(4): 666–688.

Tawney, R.H. (1942) 'The American Labour Movement', in Winter, J.M. (ed) (1979) *R.H. Tawney: The American Labour Movement and other Essays*, Brighton: Harvester Press.

Taylor, P. and Moore, S. (2015) 'Cabin crew collectivism: Labour process and the roots of mobilization', *Work, Employment and Society*, 29(1): 79–98.

Taylor, R. (2000) *The TUC: From the General Strike to New Unionism*, Basingstoke: Palgrave.

Teamsters (2019) *Who Are The Teamsters?*, https://teamster.org/about

Teddlie, C. and Tashakkori, A. (2011) 'Mixed methods research: Contemporary issues in an emerging field', in Denzin, N.K. and Lincoln, Y.S. (eds), *The SAGE Handbook of Qualitative Research*, Thousand Oaks, CA: Sage, pp 285–299.

Terry, M. (2000) *Redefining Public Sector Unionism: Unison and the Future of Trade Unions*, London: Routledge.

The Black List (2019) *Which Guild Do I Join?*, https://blcklst.com/education/wgae

The Gazette (2016) *Petitions to Wind Up (Companies)*, www. thegazette.co.uk/notice/2480215

TUC (2019) *Union Listing*, www.tuc.org.uk/unions

Tuckman, A. (2018) *Kettling the Unions: A Guide to the 2016 Trade Union Act*, Nottingham: Spokesman Books.

Turner, H.A. (1962) *Trade Union Growth Structure and Policy*, London: Allen and Unwin.

Turner, J.C. and Tajfel, H. (1986) 'The social identity theory of intergroup behavior', in Worchel, S. and Austin, W. (eds), *Psychology of Intergroup Relations* (2nd edn), Chicago: Nelson Hall, pp 7–24.

UCAC (2019) *UCAC to Discuss Devolution at Plaid Cymru Conference*, www.ucac.cymru/index.php?q=plaid+cymruandoption=com_fi nderandview=searchandlang=enandItemid=101

Undy, R. (2008) *Trade Union Merger Strategies: Purpose, Process and Performance*, Oxford: Oxford University Press.

Undy, R., Ellis, V., McCarthy, W.E.J. and Halmos, A.M. (1981) *Change in Trade Unions: The Development of the U.K. Unions Since the 1960s*, London: Hutchinson.

Unite (2013) *Community Membership*, www.unitetheunion.org/ growing-our-union/communitymembership

Visser, J. (2012) 'The rise and fall of industrial unionism', *Transfer: European Review of Labour and Research*, 18(2): 129–141.

Waddington, J. (1995) *The Politics of Bargaining: The Merger Process and British Trade Union Structural Development 1892–1987*, London: Mansell Publishing.

Walters, G. (2004) *The Professional Footballers Association: A Case-Study of Trade Union Growth (Research Paper)*, London: Birkbeck College, www.sportbusinesscentre.com/research/research-papers

Webb, S. and Webb, B. (1894) *The History of Trade Unionism*, London: Longmans.

Webb, S. and Webb, B. (1902) *Industrial Democracy*, London: Longmans.

Webb, S. and Webb, B. (1920) *The History of Trade Unionism 1666–1920*, London: Longmans.

Weber, M. (1978) 'The nature of social action', in Runciman, W.G. (ed), *]: Selections in Translation*, Cambridge: Cambridge University Press, pp 43–56.

Wen, X. and Lin, K. (2014) 'Restructuring China's state corporatist industrial relations system: The Wenling experience', *Journal of Contemporary China*, 24(94): 665–668.

Whetten, D.A. (2006) 'Albert and Whetten revisited: Strengthening the concept of organizational identity', *Journal of Management Inquiry*, 15(3): 219–234.

Whittaker, D.H. (2013) 'Japan', in Frege, C. and Kelly, J. (eds), *Comparative Employment Relations in the Global Economy*, Abingdon: Routledge, pp 245–264.

Williams, S. (2017) *Introducing Employment Relations: A Critical Approach* (4th edn), Oxford: Oxford University Press.

Willman, P., Morris, T. and Aston, B. (1993) *Union Business: Trade Union Organisation and Financial Reform in the Thatcher Years*, Cambridge: Cambridge University Press.

Wills, J. (2004) 'Trade unionism and partnership in practice: Evidence from the Barclays–Unifi Agreement', *Industrial Relations Journal*, 35(4): 329–342.

Zhu, Y., Warner, M. and Feng, T. (2011) 'Employment relations "with Chinese characteristics": The role of trade unions in China', *International Labour Review*, 150(1-2): 127–143.

Index

Note: Page numbers in *italic* type refer to figures; those in **bold** type refer to tables.